The Epitome of a Player

By

Ernest Ivy II

The Epitome of a Player
Playin Without Gettin Played

Copyright © 2008 by Ernest Ivy II

Library of Congress registration # TXU001205756/2004-10-28
First published print: 2008

ISBN-978-0-615-25635-1

All rights reserved. No part of this book may be reproduced or transmitted in any form or by any means, electronic or mechanical, including photocopying, recording or by any information storage and retrieval system, without written permission from the author, except for the inclusion of brief quotations in a review.

Book printing by Lulu Publishing Company (Lulu.com)

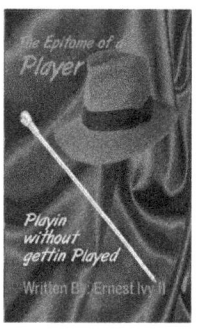

Edited By &Cover Design By:
Mick
travelingpcdoctor@yahoo.com

The Epitome of a Player

DEDICATION

This book is dedicated to the late

Samello Bledsoe Ivy

ACKNOWLEDGEMENTS

I would like to thank my son Ernest Ivy III for his help with the research and skills for formatting this book

Thank you very much Mick for your work with the graphic design and the critique for my book. Email address travelingpcdoctor@yahoo.com

Table of Contents

	Introduction	5
1	The Fundamentals of a Player	13
2	The Game	24
3	The Gentlemen of Leisure	30
4	The Man of Leisure	35
5	The Mack	41
6	The Pimp	55
7	The Lady of Leisure	62
8	The Female Non Player	70
9	The Male Non Player	79
10	Wannabes, Would have beens, Could have beens, Should have beens, Never will be's, and Maybes	86
11	Players and the Penitentiary	98
12	Players and Power	108
13	Why Women Choose Players	119
14	Why Men Become Players	133
15	Making Things Happen	141
16	The Psychology of a Players Circle	149
17	Peace and Love	160
18	Haters and Busters	162
19	Where Men Fail	167
20	Losers and Winners	174
	Summary	179
	Glossary	182
	About the Author	184

INTRODUCTION

Bodies and blood splattered on the street; while an innocent child lies on the sidewalk with a bullet in his head; and the killers are destined for hell. It has to stop! Hustlers are repeating their blunders; and the information they're dying for is in this book, to save lives all over the world. This process will formulate the epitome of a player (which means the highest level of a player or all you can be as a player in the game).

You are about to go on a maze. As a matter of fact, this will be the adventure of your life. You are about to look at women, men, and yourself in a different way.

I decided to write this self-help motivational book to help out street players (between the ages of fourteen and thirty four) in order to make a major impact on the cessation of numerous killings on the streets and in relationships. How many people look over their shoulder when they're walking down the street (depending on the neighborhood you live in)? I can imagine how many people that read this book will raise their hands and say something like "amen to that." There was a time during the sixties when the suburbs and plush areas downtown were basically free of gunfire and hard drugs. Even marijuana was scarce in those areas. The drugs and gunfire are practically dominant in major cities (and suburbs) all over the world now. Our young men are taking a bath in drugs, and then they hit the streets to play Two Gun Pete and The Two Gun Kid (but using real bullets). Those same young bucks are mentally begging for a veteran player to pull them to the side, and then feed them the information they have desperately needed (like water and air) to survive. The violence has thickened; not just on the streets, but on jobs also. The area doesn't make a difference. You either know what you're doing out there or you don't. The reality of the crowded graveyards and penitentiaries are evidence that way too many hustlers' in this tough, deadly game, are vanished or confused. I clarify that dilemma and provide a positive and respectful direction in chapter two (The Game).

And by the way ladies, I didn't forget you all either. Oh Yeah, I could picture those little halos floating around your heads while I was talking about the men, but there are many female players in this world also. Women start learning their slick hustles and tactics around the age of adolescence just like men. I have a discussion about that in the <u>Lady of Leisure</u> chapter.

The Epitome of a Player

Now wouldn't you just know it! There are plenty of men and women in life that don't choose to be called a player. That's fine. I just didn't want you nice people to feel left out of this book, so I included chapters about non-female and non-male players. What a shame, I didn't leave one stone unturned. Did you know that a great many people that's non-male and non-female players have some of the qualities of a player in their personalities? Yep! They sure do. Well, I'll simply put it like this; it would be pretty hard to find a man or woman who never had friends or associates that were players. Maybe they read a book about players or seen a movie about it. How about the discussions that the typical men will have in the groups they gather into on street corners? How about the group of women who (at the same time) run into the washroom and get into a football huddle to gossip?

I know what the men are talking about on street corners because I have been on many of those street corners with them. And I know what women are talking about because I have been in the middle of some of their football huddles on the job or the streets when they gossip.

It is impossible for someone to go through life and not learn a little information about the male and female players, and the tactics they use, because players are all over the world. Society everywhere is made up of many complex systems of manipulation, con and wit. The slow accept the circumstances and the swift make things happen. One way or the other; the personalities of hustlers will rub off to a certain degree on others, no matter what they choose to call him or her. Do you think that those who consider themselves non-male and non-female players have ever used some of those learned tactics on others? There is a good probability that they have.

I give our young people clarity on the many misconceptions of what players are and what they do. Then I have chosen to give insight, foresight, and guidance to those who made a decision to enter a very fast game while acknowledging themselves as players. It is pertinent for them to know that their final accomplishment is elevating to the epitome of a player.

Many people all over the world have the conception that players are pimps who put women on the streets to solicit dates for profit or they have several girlfriends who give them money. That is the style of some, but it is not the style for many of them. There is a difference between a pimp, mack, and man of leisure, gentleman of leisure and lady of leisure. I

Introduction

rarely run into someone who know the differences or have even heard of all those styles. I talk about all five styles in five consecutive chapters and the second chapter titled: <u>The Game</u>.

I talk about a serious game where as a man or woman has to know the in's and out's of life-along with the loop holes in order to survive on the streets or on a job. Their life, bread and butter on the table, depend on it. That's right, I said on a job. Many people think that a player is someone who is only on the streets and the game is only played out there. But that's far from the truth. The game is also played on jobs. There are many people who have to "learn the ropes" to make it easier to keep their jobs as well as surviving on the streets.

I have worked on several jobs and I recall the many complaints about how unfair management is, how co-workers play tricks on others; along with favoritism in hiring and moving up the ladder at work. There are also those complaints about some people doing more work than others, but they're on the same level. The issuing of raises is considered to be political-with certain people being favored. Don't forget about the good old complaint of how some people can call in sick a lot and get away with it. People have to learn how to play their way in and out of situations on a job in order to get the nice raise, move up the ladder; get co-workers off their back, call in sick a lot and get away with it, take long lunch breaks; and basically do just about whatever they want to do. You either learn how to play the game or accept the circumstances that's handed down to you. It's your choice.

Just like on the streets, people need to think about the information they are getting from their associates while at work. If the information you are getting is not helping you to get your way then you are communicating with the wrong people. They either don't play the game; or they don't know you well enough to give you the information you're looking for; so it's time to get rid of them and find new associates! Keep on doing that until you start getting the knowledge you need in order to help you out. It will be appropriate for you to start thinking about giving up some helpful information in order to get some help. If two people are together and one of them is doing all the benefiting; then the other one is not needed. Both parties should benefit.

I found a need to reach out to young people in this book because many of them are out there on those streets just guessing about a lot of aspects pertaining to street games; and they are dying from overdoses and gunshots. They have been doing a lot of time in jails, institutions, and penitentiaries. For that reason, I chose to discuss the different components of the players (in chapter one), which is basically their different styles, techniques, and purpose in life.

Many young people are taking to the streets because the sell of drugs bring in big, fast money. Their atmosphere is considered to be very cool. Con games are very popular, along with gambling; and the flash of having pretty women bring prostitution money to hustlers is pre-dominant. I talk about the in's and out's of street games and pimping. It's not as glamorous or as easy as it seems. When I use the phrase in's and out's; I mean have a way out, once you are in. This savvy book will save the lives of many hustlers because I break down street terminology and systems that will provide a positive direction and profitable (legal) results for the hustler on the job, the streets, or those who utilize both areas

In 1978 I got caught up in one of the inevitable circumstances of street hustler's. I was standing in front of a judge after losing a case on a robbery charge; and I got sentenced to four years in the penitentiary. I'm writing this book from my personal experience of being in the mix, around the block and back. I got credit for doing three months in Cook County Jail, then three months in the House of Correction (both in Chicago). I did three months in Joliet Processing Center and one year in Pontiac. I got three months of good time (I only had to do half of the four years), and got out January 17, 1981. I have never stepped one foot in another jail cell since then. I was twenty-seven years old when I was released. I turned twenty-eight two days later.

I was on the yard one day in Pontiac-holding a conversation with three players. We decided to break down the pimping game by defining the difference between pimps, macks, men of leisure, gentleman of leisure, and ladies of leisure, because we knew that it was a big controversy on the streets. We decided to get it straight between the four of us. We socialized enough to know that there is a major catastrophe among young players who can't (but should) get those differences correct.

There is an old saying on the streets that if you slip up and go to the penitentiary-it should only happen once. If anyone is going back and forth to the big house-they should give that process serious thought-then come up with some good answers to understand why they keep screwing up; and then make a positive change. I provide those answers in this book.

Introduction

The results of our discussion in the yard are in the first six chapters of this book. You will find it to be very interesting.

While incarcerated, I read every darn book I could get my hands on. Doing time is a learning process so that's what I did. I took what I learned (on my own time reading, with college) in Psychology, Logic, and Sociology; and then combined it with my experiences on the streets of Chicago. Now I have came up with a solution to help provide respect and equality to all women of the Earth. Way too many women have already suffered physical and mental abuse from egotistical men who don't know what they're doing. And they don't even have a clear understanding of purpose and a positive direction in life. Haven't our women put up with enough? I discovered a spiritual connection to the bond and commitment of a serious male and female relationship. I have unraveled the puzzle of the rationality behind an ordained order of the myth behind the rule over women by men. This was stated at the beginning of time when there was only one man and one woman on earth.

The misinterpretation of the word rule has disillusioned many people and has lead to the hate, prostitution, pandering, drugs, and the destruction of lives. And I mean those lives of men, women, and kids. I talk about this discovery in full detail in the chapter titled: Where Men Fail. The spiritual breakdown of rule, tells why there's a misunderstanding and mistreatment towards women by many men. Those (men) players are the biggest perpetrators that construct confusion in life by not knowing, understanding, and making appropriate adjustments to the different styles of players (and spiritual concepts). I discussed that issue in the first six chapters.

After reading the chapter titled: Where Men Fail, the average person will have to question their acknowledgement of what is, and what should have always been considered appropriate behavior in a courtship, friendship; and marriage between a man and a woman. My findings will be controversial, interesting, enlightening, and challenging, but hard to base a concrete argument against.

A close friend of mines explained the term lady of leisure to me long before I got my four-year sentence. Of course she was a professional lady of leisure herself (we didn't get along). I have discovered through my associations with other con's that there was more than one style in that

The Epitome of a Player

area. In the chapter titled: <u>The Lady of Leisure</u>, I have broken down and explained the three different styles of this woman. I went on to discuss the development of the lady of leisure in the chapter titled: <u>Where Men Fail</u>.

When I got out of Pontiac January 17, 1981, I had been very well self-educated. I became more knowledgeable in the areas of the origin of players, their different styles, and what I have considered to be the most appropriate of all the styles, which is that of the professional <u>gentleman of leisure</u>.

I became well versed and knowledgeable in the subjects that I studied in salesmanship, effective decision-making, conducting speeches, personality types and masterminding techniques. I also studied subjects that explained the-sixth sense, goal setting, negotiations, assertiveness, meditation techniques, motivation, leadership skills, and tact.... Whenever I finished one book I would start right away on a new one. I was ready for a new life and a better way of handling my business.

I got a job working in a hospital February 17, 1981. At that time I decided to put to use all the knowledge I had acquired. I changed my style from mack to the style of the man of leisure. When I got more experience in life I strived for the professional gentleman of leisure role.

While I worked at the hospital, I learned more about people who considered themselves to be non-male and non-female players. I also started realizing that there were many players who worked on a job out of their own choosing. Some of the biggest players of the game were in management. I learned that the more power a person has; the more apt they were to play the game.

There was a very suave gentleman who had a modest position at the hospital who was always telling people he was a player. He drove a stylish Cadillac, was married and owned some investment properties. He eventually left the job and moved to California. I was use to the outspoken ones that were playing the streets, but not those on a job; and he can only be categorized as a professional gentleman of leisure. And yes, players do work on jobs (contrary to what many people think). Many of them branch off into their own business or they stick with the routine that makes them comfortable. They have numerous choices, and I would hope that young people would take note of this and stop thinking that working on a job is demeaning, because that is a step in the right direction while making life changing decisions.

Introduction

The ability to get things done is <u>power</u>. If you can't make positive decisions and get positive results in your life-then you don't understand power and struggle to get ahead in life. I talk about this subject in the chapter titled: <u>Players and Power</u>. I also included a helpful chapter about making things happen, because those ideas are very complimentary to the chapter on power. I give enough ideas in that chapter to provide a realistic approach to a strong challenge in life for the player and non-player.

The shrewd knowledge in this book will help hustlers identify what category they are in and make the appropriate adjustments to be all they can be in life. Identifying yourself as a non-player is part of that process so you can be all that you can be in that area also, but do understand that people have player characteristics. How can a person function in life or survive in this world without some of those characteristics.

I realize that no matter what someone says in a book about street life and the game, there are people who are already set in their ways. The penitentiaries are never going to stop taking in those that make the same mistakes over and over every year (in other words, let it rest). I have a chapter that talks about players in the penitentiary; and I discuss how to survive once a person ends up there. I also hope that chapter will make hustlers think a little more carefully about the decisions they make in regards to whether the outcome will send them to the penitentiary if they get caught.

Life is a continuous flow of our decision making processes every second of each day. A practice of making wise decisions on a daily basis will make a huge difference in keeping extra money in your pockets, as well as, having a hard or easy life. Making a decision to love yourself as well as others is a process that adds contentment to a person's life; and that's why I talked about <u>haters</u> and <u>busters</u> in this book. Hating will rip away the inner soul and bring discontentment and disharmony in ones life. Many people will raise their eyebrow after reading that chapter, because those who have hate inside of them know who they are, and many of them are busters who will try to break up anything good in another person's life because of the hate they carry inside of them.

By now the reader can sense the extensive outlook I am expressing about a fast game with the ability to survive and provide a living for you. And for others, a family would be included. There is nothing funny about no food on the table while short on paying the bills. I provide the answers for avoiding that situation in this book. It will be up to you to make any

The Epitome of a Player

necessary adjustments. I can lead you to the water, but will you drink it? While you're reading this book you are going to explore a dimension of the subconscious that will alert and educate the hustler's conscious mind to the most shocking realities of surviving in a player's detrimental world. Nobody said the game was easy and that's ok, because it gets better with time.

    I will briefly comment on the disgrace of the people who naively added to the mass confusion and misunderstandings of categorizing, and perceiving some people as players who really are not! Just because some people dress like one, try to act like one, and may even go so far as to say they are one, don't mean a thing. I talk about this subject in detail in the chapters titled: <u>Wannabes, Could Have Beens, Would Have Beens, Should Have Beens, Never Will Be's and Maybes</u>. They are always in the way of everybody in the entire world; including themselves.

    That is one of the strong chapters that I hope will provide support for my entire book by bringing back understanding, dignity and respect, for those who honor the game, and conduct their business maturely and professionally. Now flip the page, sit back, relax and let your mind go with the flow-this is your adventure in a brand new world.

1

THE FUNDAMENTALS OF A PLAYER

The fundamentals of anything are the basis or the reason of its existence, and the rationality of its structure. In other words, there has to be a good, constructive rationality, for the existence, make up, and value of a player.

The phrase "<u>epitome of a player</u>" means: "all that one can be" as a player in this fast paced game. It is the highest level one can reach as a professional. This entire book represents that subject; but how can I go on to the next chapter (The Game) without talking about the composition of the person who has chosen a player's lifestyle? I can't.

I lost count of all the young people I passed up over the years on the streets of Chicago who had a question mark in their eyes; and I knew they were hanging out trying to be hip and cool. Such is life in the big city. There was a story in their eyes asking for help and guidance on how to get started in the fast lane. They were always too afraid to ask. They were afraid that maybe I would reject them, but they were wrong. It was typical of me to help out a young person on those streets whenever they asked. Sometimes I would volunteer my help.

One day a young player (about twenty four) came up to me and asked a question about a problem he was having with his woman who was down for him by turning dates, and any other means for bringing him money. He told me that he was suspicious of his woman spending a lot of time with another man and he was afraid she would leave him.

He asked me if he should just beat the mess out of her and go on about his business. I asked him if he had another woman to replace her if he did that. He said no. I told him that it would not be a wise decision to get rid of her, because she's the bread and butter on the table. I told him to talk it over with her and see if she keeps on bringing in money, and if she stops bringing in money; then he can knock the mess out of her, and then get rid of her.

I was only thirty-one and had only been in the mack game for ten years. If I had more experience I would have told him to simply break up the relationship without hitting her, because I learned later on in life that there were different styles that players practiced and it wasn't fair for him to be introduced to only one technique. I would have introduced him to

The Epitome of a Player

what I felt was a more relaxed style, which is that of the <u>man of leisure</u> or <u>gentleman of leisure</u>. He probably ended up knocking the mess out of his woman. I will never know, and never asked, because she was his bread and butter on the table, not mines. It simply wasn't my business to follow up on.

The point I'm making is that it's important to know why you chose to be a player, what your style is, and where you are headed in the game. You simply need to know the basic fundamentals of getting started. I need to specify this for the young people (between the ages of fourteen and thirty four) who are already on those cold hard streets; and the ones who are thinking about getting out there to try their hand.

Organizing a group of women to do whatever you ask them to do and bring you money is a business. A young buck stepping into hell (street hustle) for the first time has a lot of homework to do. You are walking a very thin line between death and the penitentiary. You need to know precisely what you're doing, and it would help tremendously if you can find a veteran in this game who will not mind spending a little of his time every now and then to help you out.

It is appropriate to give the veteran a little gift every now and then for helping you out. It can be in cash, a shirt, tie or slacks; and you will not be getting taken advantage of, because game is to be sold not told. The veteran's that help you deserve something, because it's hard to find an experienced hustler to take out the time to help you. One of the reasons is because young people in the fast lane think someone should help them out for free, but that's not one of the basic fundamentals of the game or the player. The veteran has a living to make just like you have a living to make; and one day when you turn professional someone will gladly pay you for helping him out.

It would also be very complimentary for any veterans reading this to donate a little of their time for free every now and then to help a young hustler out. It will help a lot of them stay alive and on the right track in life. Your nice and deserving blessing will come from another direction.

A pimp or mack is the employer of his women. He's the man. The ladies serve his every need; bring him cash, clothes, jewelry, food, and whatever else they find valuable to his existence. A hustler will typically choose this type of lifestyle for working independently, outside of an employer, and interacting with those who are smooth, cool, and in the mix. It's all about the glamour, prestige, fast money and a challenge; in a

The Fundamentals of a Player

dangerous game. Just the thought and effort of survival everyday is enough juice to keep the young hustlers mind riding on a high.

How nice it is when he jumps out of that cool car with three or four pretty women jumping out the car with him. All of them are dressed to the max while people admire them as they look on. The man of these ladies get acknowledged for being down in the game as a hip and in the mix dude who is on top of the world spending money like running water. He does all the fancy steps with his women at the parties; then his ladies take his coat off when entering a premise, and they put his coat on when leaving.

When he wakes up in the morning one of them runs his bath water and the other one starts cooking his breakfast. One lady will wash his body down in the bath tube-then the one who's cooking will come in, rinse him off, then towel dry him. The honey that washed him down takes over the role of cooking, preparing his plate and placing it on the table. The ladies then switch up for the purpose of getting use to their roles around the house.

They will also comb his hair and answer the phone. When he is ready to make love he decides which woman will be with him. It is never their choice to make. They will wash his clothes and iron them; after that, it will be time to clean the house and do any other chores that needs to be taken care of. The only thing he does is call the shots, manage <u>all</u> the money, and be everything he needs to be to them. If they need a listening ear he will be there. If they need someone to party with, go shopping with, watch television with, have a pillow fight with or even argue with, he is there for them. They are never alone and they rest assured that they are part of a family. It is always nice to belong to a good group of people that share common interests, especially if those people have come from broken homes with one or both parents absent for whatever the reason is.

I have just introduced you to the basic beginning stages and <u>fundamentals of a player</u>. The reason for his existence, rationality, and his structure, solely rest for power, prestige and success.

But the fundamentals don't stop there. This is an extensive process. How can I talk about the highs without talking about the lows? I can't. There is a reality to every business so never get away from that fact. There will be obstacles to rise above. You see, for all the reasons you felt this player's game was worth entering, you need to come up with all the

The Epitome of a Player

reasons on why it's time to pull out or advance to a higher level. This is true for the men and their women.

It has to be fundamentally understood that a player's lifestyle on the streets is a fast game to make fast money then pull out while using the money for investments or use your knowledge for acquiring the large sum of money you neglected to pull out of the streets with. The game will still be your life; but it has simply been taken off the streets to another area in life that calls for an elevation in education, style, and business matters.

The use of drugs has caused many players and their women to make a fantasy world out of the streets, bars, poolrooms and drug houses. They had gotten use to feeling mellow off narcotics and lost perspective of the fundamentals of the game. This has proven costly with death, big time in the penitentiary or a vegetable that use to be a person. When the man of the family gets strung out and loses perspective of the business that his game should have always been about-the entire family starts to fall apart.

The police have confiscated many cars, jewelry, cash, and homes of players. They have failed to understand the fundamentals of a style that is so common to the law that it was necessary to switch styles from the pimp or mack, to the man of leisure or gentleman of leisure. The pimp and mack game are not the kinds of business that people are expected to stay in year after year. That's why it's called the fast life. You get in, move fast, get your business taken care of fast, and then pull out or advance. It's time to switch up and elevate your style at that point and time. Don't be slow and don't be lazy. Do your homework.

It takes ten years to be a veteran in the game; but that don't mean all ten of those years have to be spent on the streets with a drug habit to go along with it. As a matter of fact, many players don't realize that they never had to start out playing the streets in the first place. I was guilty of not knowing that. It took me ten years (with time in the penitentiary included) to learn about the different styles of players, and the fact that drugs never had to be a part of the game. A humongous number of young bucks are doing drugs everyday, got one or two women in their corner, while driving a beat up car (if they got a car), and living in a run down hotel room. Then they eat lunchmeat practically everyday.

Young players have to stop equating drugs with the fast lane, and realize that it has been about them having things: like Bentley's, BMW's, Cadillac's, Condo's, and a fat bank account. It's all about them becoming

The Fundamentals of a Player

independent contractors and entrepreneurs. It's a swift lifestyle with the use of skills, intelligence and wit.

Playing the streets is the entry level for those who didn't know about all of the other styles (that are an elevation of the game) that are complimentary to their existence and all that they are about in life. They are called <u>street players</u> because the majority of their time and hustle is out on the streets.

If you are out there on the streets without the acquired knowledge and fat bank account of an experienced, down hustler; then it doesn't make a difference if you have one or two women, because it's obvious that they're bringing you crumbs with the nerve to call it money! How can they bring you a lot of money when they are getting high off drugs with most of the money before they bring you that change back? Then they have the audacity to say <u>come on daddy let's go buy some dope</u>. And that's a darn shame because you will actually take those crumbs that they call money, and go buy some dope-knowing that the rent is three months behind, the gas and lights have been shut off; and you're just that close to being put out on the streets.

At that point it's time to wake up out of that disillusioned fantasy world you created with drugs after everything else has failed. You were schooled on how to get your pimp or mack game started and the buck stopped there! No one explained it to you about how to rise above drugs and alcohol once you got hooked. Isn't it obvious by now that a little common sense goes with the territory?

Everything is not going to be laid out on a platter for the young hustler stepping into a cold hard game with no sympathy coming from your companions when you run out of money to buy more drugs. They will leave you and then love you again when you get some more money for some more drugs. Welcome to the game Mr. and Mrs. Drug addict. That's all you have accomplished if you have nothing else to show for your activities. You have only-successfully acquired-a drug habit. Did someone ever tell you that drugs were one of the fundamentals of a player? Now you know darn well nobody told you to get a drug habit! Isn't it obvious that something is wrong at this point and time? Can't you smell the coffee burning instead of the drugs cooking? Can't you read the handwriting on the wall instead of the police reading you your rights?

You screwed up by staying on the streets too long! What about the mansion, the fancy clothes, fancy cars, plenty of money; and then your

The Epitome of a Player

success as an independent contractor, or even an entrepreneur? There is supposed to be a happy ending to all the mess you put yourself through. It's up to you to clean up the mess. No one can, or will do it for you.

The game has not come to an end after losing your women, cars and money. Hold on to your dignity, player. Life is a continuous learning experience; and you will only get better, not worse. Pick up the pieces and get your program in order with the changes I introduce to you in this book. The game has just begun. You have just graduated from the school of hard knocks. It doesn't matter where you're at in life at this time, or how bad your situation may seem. You had to start from somewhere; and even though it didn't have to be the streets, it's ok. Read on.

I am going to talk about the beginning stages of the pimp and mack game for those young people who are thinking about trying their hand out in those areas. I will explain the pros and cons. By the time you finish this book you will understand what it takes to get going and to be successful in this game you chose.

This is not a typical pimp book about street game, players, and relationships after the streets are over. This is a whole new ballgame and a completely different play, where as the stage is presented with new and different characters in a new world where high society and classy living dominate the scenario. Welcome to the change you've been looking for.

Before coming into the new-it is necessary to explore the old and understand where you came from before you can really understand where you're going. So read on because this is where you came from.

You needed a decent wardrobe and money saved up in case you needed to get yourself or one of your ladies out of jail (and she would sit for awhile if she wasn't bringing in that much money). Sometimes you depended on a relative or a friend to get you out of jail when you were broke; and eventually they ran out of money and patience so you had to sit in jail for a while.

Many young men have went to jail for a few days with a nice suit on and came out with a pair of blue jeans, t shirt, and gym shoes on-because some big bully con felt that your suit would look nicer on him. Some of you didn't have your own place and your parents got tired of the drug traffic and your prostitutes running back and forth out of the house, so you had to find your own place to stay.

Many young people didn't realize that they seriously needed some burial insurance. That's right <u>burial insurance!</u> <u>Do you really think you're</u>

The Fundamentals of a Player

going to Disneyworld when you step out on those streets? Many young people hit the streets with blindfolds on; and their relatives ended up footing the bill for their funeral and burial. The average young people don't care about who will foot the bill when they irresponsibly enter a lifestyle where the penitentiary is on one side of the line and the graveyard is on the other.

And let's face it: when one of your relatives died, you either didn't have any money to help out with the expenses or you didn't give up any money if you had some, because you needed it to buy drugs! So for those who are making a happy meal out of drugs with all your money? I would suggest that you have the decency and respect to purchase funeral and burial insurance for yourself. Your loved ones will appreciate it. You are not a little kid anymore when you step in the fast lane. You are an adult so be responsible.

The majority of you carried a gun around and kept it in your car, because the streets are full of drug addicts and stick up men. When I was out there playing the streets my own buddies told me that if I don't start carrying a gun they was going to stick me up one day and take my money. I laughed, but they didn't. At that point I realized they were serious.

They said it was nothing against me, but I was aware that they were doing hard drugs and everyone is a target when they get high, broke, and want more drugs. I said ok, I would get a gun. I went out and bought me a gun the next day-then I came to the spot where they hung out at and flashed my gun, and said: "I'm packing now." They said ok, and never brought up the subject again. I had a good mind to stick all of them up just for G.P (general purposes), but I was true to the game and had more honor than that.

All of you on the streets got high on hard drugs like heroin, cocaine, cough syrup, valiums, speed, marijuana, alcohol, and so on. You got high on anything that wasn't nailed down and ended up going to a rehabilitation program or staying lost in the game until your life was practically that of a vegetable.

I have never heard of a person successful at using hard drugs and not getting hooked; but if you hear of such a person please let me know so that both of us will know, because you will have definitely came up with a phenomenal person.

The obviously, over crowded jail cells and penitentiaries, are proof that young people are not open-minded about the possibility of doing a

The Epitome of a Player

few years or life behind bars. They actually think that they are invincible. Maybe someone can tell me why young people believe death or the jail cells will pass them by? What's the difference between you and me? You bleed just like me and you can fit in a cell just like me.

Not only did your relatives get you out of jail, they had to foot the bill to pay for your attorney also. Now is the time for me to take you from where you've been to where you should be headed if you want to play the game for real, and bring bank and success into your program. The man of leisure and gentleman of leisure are typically not found on the streets. You will need to stay in school in order to practice that style, because you will be dealing with high-tech advanced game.

Those who dropped out of school made a big mistake. They were lost in their thoughts and lost in the game! The young bucks headed for the streets looking for knowledge because game is knowledge, but what was the purpose of dropping out of school if game is knowledge? Didn't you go out the door backwards when you left the school system that was providing all the knowledge you needed for success in life? Game is everywhere. It's out on the streets, in schools, libraries, books and tapes. What the heck were you thinking about when you dropped out? Well, all right, it's ok today. Just put the dog gone blunt down. You're back on the right track now. You are about to learn how to work smarter and not harder.

As for the ladies of the night and those who don't even care what time of the day it is, I am pleased to tell all of you that it's ok to give up prostitution. For some strange reason many women have gotten the impression that street hustle is a lifetime self-employed career (so give me a break). Well, just like the pimp and mack game is fast and temporary, the solicitation for dates and finance is the same fast and short-lived hustle (wake up). At some point it's time to switch up and elevate her style to the <u>professional lady of leisure</u>.

The lady of leisure don't play the streets and don't need to turn dates, because she reached the epitome of a player's lifestyle to be all that she was meant to be in the game (and extend her chances for a long life). Your body and mind has got to be tired after all these years on the streets. Something has been registering in your thoughts that maybe you're doing something out of pocket at this point and time. And you know what? You are right! You have had one foot in the Twilight Zone & one foot in the Outer Limits way too long. You either didn't know about the different styles of the lady of leisure, or you simply couldn't adjust to it at the time you were in-between two worlds. Well, it's ok to give that change another try and elevate your style and game. The Lady of Leisure chapter will help you out.

Now I need to talk about the fundamental values and skills for dealing with rejection in this fast paced game. This is an area where thousands and thousands of young men are way out in left field. Even as I type this manuscript I am hearing about young players saying mean words to women who won't speak sometimes when they walk by a young man that speaks to them. It is inappropriate to curse her out or say mean words to her because you never know what's on a woman's mind when she walks by. Women do not have to rehearse on how they will speak to you young men before they leave their homes. The ladies don't owe us men anything so stop acting as if they do

Many of you cool young men have not been schooled and are ranking the game and yourselves with elicit behavior. If a young lady doesn't speak then the young player should simply say something like: have a nice day anyway. She may speak the next time and if she doesn't then don't worry about it. Focus on the other young women walking by.

Some women don't speak because they are mad at their mothers or fathers or their sleazy boyfriends. Sometimes they might simply be wore out from not getting enough sleep last night for whatever the reason is; and if you haven't figured this out yet; you are not going to be the icing on the cake for every woman you meet (and so what!). Take it like a man and be understanding, polite, and professional (another one is on the way).

It is also inappropriate for a young man to walk up to a young lady he don't know and grab her hand while trying to walk and talk to her. Are you mad man of the year? You have to earn the right to put your hands on a woman! This game calls for respect and professionalism. Young players should not hang out on those streets acting like they are desperate for a conversation and relationship with a young lady. Be cool, smooth, calm and collective. Keep your hands off the women until you get to know them. They will let you know in some mature form or fashion when it's all right for you to put those slick hands on them; and be delicate when that happens. Be a sweet mack. Touch her softly and squeeze her gently. She will need to understand that you're a man who knows how to tease, please, and completely satisfy a woman.

The Epitome of a Player

It has been the style of the pimp and mack to beat their women when they are considered to come home with that short money or they are rude and impolite. I would like to point out that the style of the pimp and the mack is outdated, brutal and unnecessary. If players have to go through all those changes with women-then it's a darn good thing I wrote this book. They are working too hard for their money. They needed to hear it from somewhere so why not me. The relationship is not worth all that sweat and true players don't work like that (unless someone educated you on the game in a boxing ring). Let her go and replace her with someone else who will cooperate (you're not her therapist). And better yet, just switch to the elevated style of the gentleman of leisure who has only one woman and choose to make his own money. Who in this world is going to make you the kind of money you need anyway (without going through a hell of a lot of changes)? Some play the game for the sport of it.

Many players are intelligent enough to make their own money. They don't need the security that many women give to the man's image and ego. Many pimps and macks that leave the game alone and get married will carry that brutal treatment of beating his wife like he did the women in his family of sporting ladies.

This player's game was never meant to be a system where women are beaten like cats, dogs and cows (don't sweat it). My chapter on <u>Where Men Fail</u> will give more details on how men got off on the wrong track with relationships. Something has to make sense when I say this brutal style has been going on way too long! Nothing stays the same in life. Things change and so do styles. Many men actually have to do an about face and update their entire outlook and viewpoint about a relationship with a woman. There are too many shelters filled up by women who have been battered and threatened by men. I think something is wrong with that picture.

It is my belief that young girls and boys should do role playing in grammar schools around the age of eleven and twelve, to help them develop discipline when having a disagreement or dispute between each other. It is essential for young people to learn at an early age that all relationships will not work out. They have to understand that there will be occasional arguments, frustrations, disagreements and dissatisfactions in the courtship, friendships and marriage, because many take things to the extreme.

The Fundamentals of a Player

I'm putting an emphasis on the fact that it is essential for young hustlers to understand and be able to explain the difference between a pimp, mack, man of leisure, gentleman of leisure and lady of leisure. The breakdown and explanation of those styles are a necessary part of the fundamentals of a player (it is very appropriate to look and sound like the professional he is in the game).

Now that I have spoken on the beginning stages of a player's fundamentals in the game, it is time for me to talk about the very nature, act, and reason for the professional development of these fundamentals. It's called **the game.**

2

THE GAME

Sad to say, I have heard of and witnessed numerous young bucks that have come out of the crib (house) with no idea of what to get into. This means they have not been schooled on the organization, innovation, marketing and preciseness of ideas (a hustler use to make money) called the game. This prepared system (before coming out the door) is mandatory for the present street players (and more elevated styles) to understand and implement successfully.

I am a firm believer that it's good to have a positive direction in life. In other words, it's good to know positively just what the heck you are doing on the streets in the first place. If you wake up in the morning and get out of bed not knowing what in the world you're going to get into that day, I would suggest that you decide to lay back down and think of something constructive to do on that day. If you don't, your buddies will think of something for the both of you (which is scary), and the results may not turn out so well.

I remember too many days when I would wake up, get myself together, go outside, run into one of my buddies; and this is how the conversation usually went:

Me: What's up?

Him: Oh, nothing much, what's up with you?

Me: Oh, nothing much, I just thought I'd come outside and see what I can get into.

I need to stop right there. Neither one of us had any business being out of bed yet. The quickest way for young people to get into trouble is to come outside with no idea of what the heck they're going to do today; because eventually someone will think of something off the back of his neck and that could be the first big step into the twilight zone (and many stay there).

Now I will get to my point. I just went over the fundamentals of a player and now I need to go over the plan of action. And I'm not talking

The Game

about just kicking it! I'm talking about a definite plan, idea, thought or quota on what you're going to do that day before you get out of bed. This means (before you go to bed at night) you will need a desk planner or notebook paper or an index card to jot down your plans for the next day. Once this takes place you are organized and ready to play the <u>game</u>!

I will start out with a few definitions of the word game that's taken from Webster's II New Riverside Dictionary. 1. <u>A set of rules completely specifying a competition.</u> 2. <u>A competitive activity.</u> 3. <u>The equipment needed for playing certain games.</u> 4. <u>A calculated action or approach.</u> I will stop there.

When I put those four definitions together I come up with: <u>a set of rules for competitive activity that</u> <u>includes necessary equipment for the use of a calculated action or approach</u>. As I stated in chapter one; make sure you understand why you chose a players game and be prepared each day to move toward the goal you have set for yourself. Your plan of action should be written down or at least understood before the next day. And for that reason it is time for me to get to the technicalities of the game.

The technicalities of the game are basically your <u>techniques,</u> which are <u>systematic procedures by which complex tasks are accomplished</u>. The technicalities of the mack are one phase of the game I'm about to discuss; and after that, I will discuss other phases of the game.

The word <u>mack</u> (in a player's game) is slang for <u>the conversation used to entice a woman to solicit dates and use any other means to bring money to the player</u>. I'm about to go over a ten step-system (game) used by pimps and macks that are basically outdated. I'm taking young people back into time-to understand how things were and what direction they should be headed in now.

1. The player would decide how many women to start out with. One to three women would be the normal average percentage.

2. It was never a good decision to pick a woman that was obviously deceitful. Some players think they can work with any woman they meet and that's a mistake because many women are on an entirely different page than many men. The player had to make sure they were flipping the same script or was she all for herself. You could be a partner and share ideas with a woman like that, but never try

The Epitome of a Player

to include her in your family unless she shows one hundred percent loyalty to you.

3. The player would pick out a bottom woman (the fastest and most loyal of all the ladies) to collect the money from the other ladies as well as manage them when the players are not available to do so.

4. They usually lived in their own apartment or house by themselves. There would be too much jealousy if the players lived with one or more of his women. And if the police ever raided the apartment it would be too easy to connect them to their women.

5. It was the players' responsibility to purchase drugs for the family. Many men made the typical mistake of allowing themselves and their women to get hooked on drugs. That sent the family on the way down.

6. Players had to be educated and disciplined enough to manage all the money and the bills. It was not the ladies role to do that. Drugs would get in the way and made money management difficult.

7. It was extremely difficult for them to have a bank account unless they purchased real estate or some other form of business to justify their income. And the police would still take their property and merchandise if the players are suspected of illegal activity.

8. The police knew who the players and their families were, so all of them were prepared to go to jail every now and then; and pay for attorney fees also.

9. The family would periodically relocate because it was never a good idea to live in one area a long time doing illegal activity.

10. The flaw behind this outdated system; is that the players and their ladies were sweating themselves in a game that was meant to be smooth and relaxing. How can you relax with the police breathing down your back and dope addicts trying to rob or kill you for your drugs and money? How could you relax going back and forth out

of jail cells, fighting a drug habit, constantly spending money on attorneys and constantly moving around from one neighborhood to another? It's time to update your game. I didn't list those ten steps in order for young bucks in the game to make a choice of calling their friends on the phone and talk about a pimp's game plan.

I wrote it to show how hustlers would put their ideas down on paper in order to have a definite plan of action, along with the fact that those played out plans have been erroneous, unnecessary and outdated. If you're using those techniques it's time to reorganize your game plan and get your house in order player. Take those old pimp books and movies to the garbage can where they belong.

Being cool, hip, and recognized in the fast lane has always been equated to dangerous decisions in many cases during teenage years on through the thirties and forties. We as teens (including me when I was a teenager) have basically gone out the door backwards with misinformation and trying our best to identify with our friends. For instance; teens have always equated coolness and maturity to smoking cigarettes, drinking, and smoking marijuana. Eventually they would start taking speed and smoking hash. Then cocaine and heroin took over.

You were not considered to be in the mix if you didn't hang out with the people who used drugs. Our friends were considered to be weak if they died from an overdose of pills or other forms of drug use. So the party and booze kept on going. Where did the game plan come in? What about legal ventures to acquire the big house, nice cars and other luxurious desires of success?

There is another world out there besides the one my peers and I entered during our youth. We didn't know there was a circle of players (women and men) who dressed nice, talked nice, was cool, calm and collected; living a lifestyle that was absent of drugs. In many cases a lot of them don't even smoke cigarettes. Now that sounds like a good system for living a longer and more relaxed lifestyle.

<u>The gentleman of leisure, man of leisure, and lady of leisure lifestyles</u> are professional levels in the game. They have learned to enjoy life absent of the pitfalls and errors of players in the past-who worked an outdated system for survival and acknowledgement in the fast lane. The following ten steps is a new game plan for those who are ready to move up

The Epitome of a Player

to the next level. It's all about being more professional and responsible with their decision-making.

1. Read the next chapters on the different styles of players very good and more than once if necessary. The styles are new to many young people on the streets and they deserve a right to know about them in order to make the appropriate adjustments.

2. It will take a continuous flow of educational programs to make necessary changes that are appropriate for advancements so get back in school fast if you dropped out and go to college or a trade school after high school.

3. Try and find an experienced veteran in the game that will not mind giving you some sound advice. And give the veteran a small gift of appreciation every now and then if you can.

4. It's wise to work a regular 9 to 5 job until you decide what career you want to venture off into. Typical players (no matter who they are) worked on 9 to 5 jobs before, and some of them still do so out of choice.

5. Get to a drug treatment center if you are hooked on drugs and alcohol. You will need a clear head to elevate your game. You will still enjoy your music and many other forms of entertainment like going out to the parties and to the movies. Roller-skating, bowling, swimming and picnics; will still interest you too.

6. You will need to get readjustment counseling after going to a drug treatment center. A lifestyle of drugs is one thing and a lifestyle without drugs is a whole new ballgame. Don't try to do it without counseling.

7. You will also need readjustment counseling if you haven't been out of the penitentiary a long time or you are about to get out of the penitentiary. Many people make the same mistakes with drugs and crime-then end up doing time behind bars again. There won't be anybody telling the convicts they need readjustment counseling

The Game

after doing time, so take this wise advice and make appropriate changes to survive in society this time around.

8. It will be necessary for numerous people to move to a different neighborhood or city to get away from old associates and meet new people who have learned to live and enjoy life without the use of drugs.

9. Be patient with life and don't look for an overnight change. New adjustments take time. Expect success and start a savings program.

10. Call somebody up on the phone right now or go by their house if you know they are wise, responsible, and capable of giving you sound advice and moral support while making this change.

You are now ready to play a new game. It is the first step to an elevated lifestyle and system for success in life. Your friends and relatives will be surprised and happy with your new standards of living. If you think long you think wrong. Make that move right now to get the ball rolling and flip to the next page to read about the gentleman of leisure (who is at the highest level of a player's game).

The Epitome of a Player

3

THE GENTLEMAN OF LEISURE

I made this the first chapter out of the five different styles I'm about to discuss because I didn't want to keep the readers (especially the young people) in suspense about the highest level of the players game; and that level is the <u>professional gentleman of leisure</u>.

This is a very complex topic that's not easy to explain. It may not be understood typically-or adapted to-without many complications. The reason why I say this is because there is an extensive learning process that goes along with this style. For those who don't like picking up many books to read and study, it can be a very diverse and grinding change. A high school education will not be enough to master the style of this high society and luxurious living player. Some college (or a trade) along with self-education will be necessary just to get started; and the learning process never stops. You can very easily get left behind in a circle where players at this level continue their education in the form of college, trade schools, some good work shops, the library, educational tapes, home study courses, and networking through computers and mastermind groups.

These are some of the definitions of the word <u>gentleman</u> that's taken out of Webster's II New Riverside University Dictionary: 1. A man of gentle or noble birth; or superior social position. 2. A polite, gracious, or considerate man having high standards of propriety or correct behavior. 3. A man of independent means who does not or need not work. 4. A man who considers manual labor to be beneath him.

All the other styles of players are the sugar in the cake, but the gentleman of leisure is the entire cake. In other words, the game is not complete without his style. This is a gentleman who has made a decision to control his own destiny without the risks that goes along with street hustle. In many cases he started out on the streets like many other players in the game, but acknowledged the sweat in those styles and rose above it all. His style is the <u>epitome of a player</u>!

That is the point of this entire book (along with saving lives). I want to take those who are ready for elevation in the game to the <u>gentleman of leisure</u> level and keep you there. There is no turning back or complaining about how much you will have to learn. It was for you to understand the provisions of the fast lane when you stepped in the mess so either get busy or step aside. This is a man's game and a strong game; it is not for the weak, weary, and lame. There are always adjustments to make in life, especially that of the gentleman's lifestyle.

When I have taken out the time to school young people on the gentleman of leisure style-I always tell them that they need a balance in their life-style that's physically, mentally, emotionally, and spiritually. This is where the uniqueness and complexity of this style comes in at; because many pimps, and the macks, don't practice spiritual and physical balance. Many of them will pass out if they jog one block. They have very little understanding of their existence and purpose in life.

I always suggest to young players that they spend 25 percent of their time <u>reading</u> for mental development, 25 percent of their time for emotional development (<u>working, time with family, friends, meditation, relaxing and sleep</u>), 25 percent of their time <u>exercising</u> (for physical balance), and then 25 percent of their time spent on <u>spiritual balance</u> (communicating with the associates who can share their ideas, thoughts, knowledge and experience in that area). It is impossible to implement the gentleman's styles without that balance because something will be missing in your life. You will lack peace of mind and positive decision-making skills in your bout for a successful, rewarding lifestyle.

It is appropriate to write down on a sheet of paper-where you feel you're at in life (percentage wise) physically, mentally, emotionally and spiritually, until the balance is 25 percent in each area. In other words, if someone writes down on paper that they spend about fifty percent of their time for mental development, and about fifty percent of their time for emotional balance, I would be concerned about their physical health and their lack of understanding about who they are as a human being and their purpose in life (spiritual balance).

There are too many young people walking around talking about; <u>I got to find myself</u>. Now, I definitely have to regain my composure behind that thought. How many darn years do you need to be on earth before you know who you are? Don't jack your slacks and mack in a woman's face talking about you're a player, then later on tell her that you got to find yourself! You just lost your player status with her, so put a freeze on it. Spiritual knowledge is not square game. There is no such thing as square game. Game is knowledge (and knowledge is game) no matter what the knowledge is about.

The Epitome of a Player

Spiritual and physical balance is the main area where pimps and macks have failed to develop themselves in the past. They continue using an old, rusty, outdated pimping style that only caused them to sweat themselves-then rank the game to the point of confusion. This tired, played out, rusty style, has created confusion, and misled people who thought that was the style of all players in the game.

There are legitimate styles and systems for professionals in this fast lane. Drugs, along with a lack of knowledge about the appropriate approach taken to a player's game and lifestyle, have been the downfall faced by many hustlers. Some cheap wine, marijuana, and sex with different women, were all it took to get a young person reminiscing about the ladies bringing him plenty of fast money. They pictured themselves driving a nice big fancy car, and wearing expensive clothes and jewelry. Maybe some of their buddies gave them a pimp book to read and that's the extent of their knowledge.

Many of these imposters don't even have a high school diploma. They really seem to think that a player's lifestyle is supposed to be an uneducated approach to success. Many of them don't even do well with women so they turn to drug dealing, con, burglary; and eventually armed robbery when they need money to feed their drug habit. Nobody ever said that drugs were an intellectual approach to success in the fast lane. It was simply assumed that drugs went with the territory.

There are men who classify themselves as gentlemen of leisure's, but in actuality, are men of leisure's who are in transition of moving up to the gentlemen of leisure style; if they survive the streets and drugs. The true gentleman of leisure has risen above drugs and illegal activity. He has formulated into a good role model for young people throughout the world. There is dignity, prestige, and honor, at that level of a player's game. Young people have a right to know about that style in order to make better choices about what they want to be in life.

It will be pretty tough for the young person who is on the streets practicing the styles of pimp or mack, to change his style over to the gentleman of leisure, because change is not easy. Being successful in life is symbolic of a person drowning, who can't swim, and is flapping his hands wildly to stay on top of the water because he wants to live.

You are that person flapping his hands when you step in the fast lane. You need the desire to live and succeed in life just that bad in order to make it. You can never stop flapping your hands because if you do you

The Gentlemen of Leisure

will die. Choose to live right now. Keep on trying and go over the ten-step process again that I discussed in the chapter titled: The Game. I listed ten positive approaches to change and success at the end of that chapter.

Remember, there is a physiological change that is basically the uncomfortable feeling of living out your life without the alcohol, drugs, and cigarettes. Anybody who has tried to give up one, two, or all three of those bad habits, knows how difficult the process can be. That's simply one of the challenges of success. It's not so easy making it on or off the streets, but it's much wiser to choose the path with less repercussions.

The pimp or the mack making this change would help themselves by talking to a wise counselor who understands physiology-which is the biological science of the essential and typical life processes, functions and activities. That would help make the change from one lifestyle to another much more bearable.

The main point for you to understand is that change doesn't come overnight; but it does happen when you keep on trying. It wouldn't take long for you to become positive role models for your own children and other young people who watch how you live your life.

Remember, there are many young people who come from broken homes with one or both parents missing, so they will use your lifestyle as a role model for theirs. Why lead them to destruction when you can reap the blessings behind providing a better lifestyle for yourself and those who are watching you?

Now I will talk about the understanding of the title gentlemen of leisure and how that relates to his relationship with women. If you divide the word <u>gentleman</u>, you have a gentle man. The term gentle is symbolic of how he treats his women. The term man is symbolic of his strength and maturity in relationships with women and when conducting legitimate business. When you add leisure to those two symbolic terms, you have a person who is a gentle man (with the ladies) that conducts his business how he wants to do it, and when he gets ready to do it. He is basically an entrepreneur or an independent contractor. I have stated earlier that some gentlemen of leisure's would work for others out of choice, because they are making good money with flexibility on their good jobs, in their lives, and are satisfied with their careers.

The <u>gentleman player</u> can be firm with his women whenever it is necessary; but he basically understands and then applies proper etiquette and language when interacting, and conducting business with the ladies.

The Epitome of a Player

Many of the gentleman players are married men with successful and stable careers. The only time you will run into one on the streets with a family of women who solicit dates for money to bring to him is when he gets bored with his lifestyle and the street hustle intrigues him at that time.

Some gentleman players hit the streets again when an upcoming lady of leisure gives him a nice piece of cash that he couldn't refuse. He will also accept a couple of her girlfriends into the family. But, as I said before, it is rare when that happens because the professional gentleman of leisure is in a high society atmosphere and is typically not found hanging out with street hustlers who participate in an outdated pimp and mack style.

The true gentleman player will never hit his woman. He has risen above that kind of brutal-cave man behavior. Why sweat himself and his style? He has mastered the tough art of effective communication, finesse, and patience. That doesn't mean he can't or will not give a woman a good argument because he can and will; it simply means that he exercise an enormous amount of maturity and self control in order to avoid physical contact. It is the mark of a suave professional to avoid what's unnecessary in relationships, as well as business dealings.

He is a shrewd businessman who is a quick thinker. He has great concentration in any situation. What sets him apart from ordinary players is his ability to take practically any business venture and turn it into cash. He acknowledge people in various places of employment who can be an asset to his career; like bankers, real estate contractors, and other investors who may do partnerships with him.

His business contacts are basically players themselves. They all have their way of recognizing each other by their demeanor and shrewd business dealings. The gentleman players will always have a constant flow of good ideas and projects to work on. Their continuous self-education and networking pays off. They don't wait for things to happen, <u>they create and make things happen</u>. They are the playmakers and doers in society. If you ever want to get something done and get it done right, just ask the busy person who is the <u>gentleman of leisure</u>.

4

THE MAN OF LEISURE

I believed that it was necessary to write this chapter next because of the massive similarity and complexity of each style. I stated in the previous chapter that the gentleman of leisure is typically a married man who is experienced and settled in life. The man of leisure is usually not married, he may do drugs lightly, and he is tougher on women than the gentleman of leisure. Both of them are the same in intellect, success, and a high society network.

Marriage is often the final stage of maturity and balance in this high-class, high tech, advanced style. The gentleman of leisure doesn't need, and is not interested in multiple relationships with women anymore. Before he reached that level he was at the third level of the game that is the subject of <u>The Man of Leisure</u> chapter.

The pimp's style is the beginning stages of the game and the mack is at the second level. The reason why, is because both of them lay down the majority of their hustle on the streets. This mean the risks that they take in life are more costly and dangerous; because of the drug use and illegal activities of pandering, credit card fraud, check fraud, boosting, con, and the list goes on.

The man of leisure, in many cases, starts out as a mack before changing over to the man of leisure style. The gentleman of leisure style is next (if he last that long). As I said before, many young people have not been aware of the different styles of players; for that reason, they start out on the streets with the styles that are most common (the pimp and mack) to them.

The man of leisure is a player who has elevated his style off the streets, but is typically not married. He simply is not ready for that. In many cases he has risen above drugs, alcohol and cigarettes; but some of them are still struggling with those ill-advised substances because they are hard habits to kick.

There is no word called <u>gentle</u> in the title of man of leisure. He is a man with the ladies but not gentle. He is still at the level of whacking a woman about saying the wrong thing out of her mouth that's disrespectful and inappropriate towards his status and profile. It hasn't been that long

The Epitome of a Player

since he switched from the second level of elevation (the mack). It takes time to get rid of brutality.

His intent is to work on his professionalism and intellect to the point of not whacking a woman at all. Change takes time. He does not organize a family of women to bring him money. He is capable of producing his own income and prefers to do so just like the gentleman of leisure. He is very intelligent, believes in continuing his education, and typically works as an independent contractor or entrepreneur. There are some in his category who prefer to work for someone else if the pay is good, the job is prestigious, and they have flexibility.

It is practically impossible for a young person to step into the fast lane for the first time and present himself as a gentleman of leisure or man of leisure. An excellent, educated mind, along with reasonable material possessions goes along with those elite styles. That usually takes time. It depends on the circle he's in, and <u>if his peers feel that he is qualified to represent one of those titles</u>. It is highly inappropriate and disrespectful for a player to tag a title on himself without the education, skills, and material possessions to back him up. Be true to yourself and the game will be true to you. Don't front. Be real.

Many teenagers don't stay in school long enough or read enough books (for self education) in order to understand and appreciate a higher level of education, which leads to an elevation in a player's game. I have been in many neighborhoods and have listened to numerous conversations of teenagers who understand that game is simply knowledge. So why are they dropping out of school? I mentioned that subject once in this book, but it has to sink into the minds of young people so I'm bringing that phrase up again. Stop thinking that all game comes from the streets. Game is everywhere. It's found in high schools, colleges, trade schools, libraries, workshops, educational tapes, various seminars, book clubs, magazines, newspapers, chess clubs, and interacting with the other professionals who continue their education and network.

Even as I write this book I am running into many hustlers who have left street hustling and drugs alone (and many were not hustling, they were just drug users). Now they are wondering what their next approach to life is when it comes to living standards, a tough job market, and paying bills. Many of them are looking for sincere love with a woman, but don't have a decent job (some don't have a job at all) or any money saved up. This is the wake up call for those types of men. A woman doesn't want to

The Man of Leisure

live in a run down apartment with two thousand roaches. Then to top it off you're struggling to make ends meet. And what about the cold cuts you're stuffing down your throat with stale bread and water? You are either too lazy to work or don't have enough sense to realize that money goes along with love. Stop thinking that a woman is suppose to accept you as you are. That's not love, that's madness. The cost of living is too high (and getting higher) for that kind of insane thinking. Of course the woman love you, but you two will need to be able to pay bills, take care of the kids, go out a lot, take vacations, wear decent clothes, pay for your continued education, afford the cost of health care; and have money saved up for emergencies. In other words, <u>get a life</u>. Love will not pay for all that!

Many men didn't mind hustling their rear end off to come up with money to buy drugs; but since they're not getting high anymore they want a woman to just accept them as they are. Get off the pity wagon (it's over crowded), and step into the real world. We men worked our butt off to come up with a fat bankroll, a boss car, slick clothes, and a smoking crib in order to get acknowledged as a bonafide player. What happened to you?

We were wheeling and dealing with drugs and in the mix, but many of us will start acting as If that kind of hustle is over with now that the drugs and streets have played out with us. Getting rid of the illicit substances and illegal activities is fine, but the hard work is never over with. Even if a man has a woman who could really care less about material possessions; it has still got to register in the man's mind that health care cost is high, taking care of the kids will be expensive, and saving up some money for retirement and future unexpected emergencies is also necessary (especially if you're paying for the expenses of a used car that has a lot of problems).

In the majority of cases hustlers have to go back to the basics. In other words, they have to start from the time they dropped out of school and get their G.E.D. or high school diploma. There is an old saying that has been floating around the streets, penitentiaries and jailhouses for many years. That old saying is that; in order for a person to make it in life he has to do certain things that he never liked to do until he find all the reasons on why he does like it. In order to help many of those people get hungry for success I'm going to list ten reasons to help motivate them to do what it takes to make it in life; even when they have to do certain things they were never interested in. This goes on until they do get interested and really feel good on the inside about their progress.

The Epitome of a Player

1. You will sincerely feel better about yourself as a strong person and bonafide hustler in life when you go back to school and get your G.E.D. or high school diploma.

2. You will meet more down players in the game at that level and also realize that they too, believe in continuing their education and reading lots of books.

3. You will be adequately preparing yourself for a more disciplined and rewarding lifestyle.

4. By picking out subjects that you like to read about (such as sports, salesmanship; investments, cars, boats, airplanes, fiction; non-fiction, computers, comedy, and the list goes on) it will be easy to start liking it; then you will build up your self-esteem, confidence and intellect.

5. It will be a big step in finding a better job and eventually becoming an independent contractor or entrepreneur if you desire.

6. You will be a positive role model for your kids, other people's kids, and society as a whole. Most important of all, you should do it for yourself.

7. You will stand a good chance of becoming a professional athlete, musician, actor, artist, or whatever your dream may be.

8. You can learn how to invest money in real estate, stocks, bonds, commodities, insurance, and even organize your own partnerships.

9. You will eventually realize how close you are to buying that nice car, boat, clothes, airplane, real estate, and even have a secure future for your family.

10. You won't have to worry about the stress of doing illegal activities, going to jails, penitentiaries, and getting hooked on drugs. Then you will have to get unhooked off drugs and spend lots of money

on attorneys to get you out of trouble. You will be able to take that money and save it. Your family members will be proud of you and you will be proud of yourself.

This is the stage where a transformation begins to take place. From now on when you look in the mirror day after day you will start seeing a new person. Your positivism will start to rise and your motivation will be on full blast. When people run into the information in the ten steps I just mentioned, it will become a way of life for them. They'll start realizing that those puzzling thoughts are turning into their goals, direction, and eventually the results they have been looking for, which lead to success.

Now a new figure of a person has emerged as he looks back on the lifestyle he lived as a pimp or mack. He realizes that he never needed to be physically abusive with the women he had. Lack of experience and lack of knowledge made that happen. He doesn't walk the same, talk the same, or wear the pimp or mack style anymore. A charismatic magnitude about his personality that draws people to him, has taken over his life and a newly found confidence controls his destiny. The streets are behind him. His new environment consists of those people who are in schools, workshops, libraries, mastermind groups; partnerships, seminars, and career oriented establishments. A giant of a person starts to emerge with the strength and self-assuredness that comes from his newly and established balance in life; physically, mentally, emotionally and spiritually.

At this point he walks by a group of people in the neighborhood who look at him in amazement because they see the new changes. He then walks into his home and look in the full-length mirror to see the new, stylish, professional figure of the man of leisure.

He is a stud with great, remarkable intellect. Macho could easily become his middle name. His motivation has soared so high that he truly knows that nothing can stop him from being successful in life. Adversity doesn't faze him at all. Here is a man that can move mountains, swim the deepest sea and cross the hottest desert. He eats bullets for breakfast, hand grenades for lunch and torpedos for dinner. Unstoppable is the strong man who has been through the grind and grilling effects of street life and hustle. He is typically not interested in marriage and raising a family like the gentleman of leisure. The thought crosses his mind occasionally. The stability of living in one area for a long time doesn't interest him. He moves around from one city to the next taking care of his business. He will only be in one certain area (living) for several years if there is business involved and a lot of money is at stake.

Many of the men of leisure will struggle with drugs and alcohol because the elevation from the style of the mack is typically new and the physiological adjustment takes time. The gentleman of leisure has either given up those substances for a good number of years (about three years at least) or never started using them at all. In either case he is above that issue.

The man of leisure has elevated his style to the third level of the game. This means he is well on his way to the fourth and highest level, the professional gentleman of leisure. The high society lifestyle goes along with it. He has earned the respect of his peers, family, and friends. Now he is ready to play the game with the heavy hitters.

5
THE MACK

I remember when I was sixteen years old living on the southeast side of Chicago during a period of time when everybody in my circle was trying to avoid a certain young man who could talk someone out of the shirt on his back (such is the mack). He would always ask if you would let him have a little change. One day he asked me for some change and after giving him money in the past I was determined not to let him have his way this time. I said no and kept on walking. But he kept walking right beside me and continued talking about the change and all the reasons on why he needed it. Well, I was still determined not to give it to him so I yelled at him and sent a few cursing words his way. To my amazement he put a calm smile on his face and said ok, and thank you anyway. He never even lost his composure, but I walked away with my head all messed up from anger, frustration and disgust.

How could I allow myself to get all hyped up when he handled the situation so professional? I talked to some homeboys about it and to my amazement again, they experienced the same predicament with him. They said that he was collecting money from women and men. It didn't matter who you were. He was doing well financially because of it. Then they told me that every now and then they would just reach in their pocket and pull out a little change and give it to him. When they saw him again; they tell him that they already gave him some money. He would say ok and leave. I thought it was a good idea and it worked after I tried it.

I have just introduced you to a young mack. He has an astounding gift of gab. People will pay him to just go away. He talks to good and seldom loses his cool. He is a professional. I don't know what happen to him. I heard that he organized a family of women and was doing well financially with them. It was said that he left our area and started moving around to different cities. No one knows what happened to him from there. He simply was not in our circle anymore. The players who are that fast and advanced never stay in the same circle they grew up in. I have seen it happen on many occasions. They will out grow the circle and start moving from neighborhood to neighborhood, and then from city to city.

The example I have just given is how a mack starts out before he organizes a family of women. The old pimp books and pimp movies don't exhibit that part of a player's life. They start out with the players and their

The Epitome of a Player

women; and then leave out their childhoods (which lead young people to imagine them as being a pimp, mack... over night). On the contrary, the development of a player is an extensive process. A young man typically cultivates the gift of gab (gift of being an exceptional conversationalist) before the family of women is organized. Now I will discuss a few of the techniques on how they get started.

I was not that fancy of a talker during my teenage years and I was swiftly put on the spot to learn fast, but that didn't happen overnight. One of the most interesting techniques a friend taught me was called a talking contest. The object was for one person to start talking about anything he chose. It didn't matter if the conversation was boring or not. He had to talk continuously without a pause in his words. When he did pause the other person had the right to cut in and start talking as long as he could. He could not pause and he could also talk about any subject he desired. Sometimes one person would talk for one or two hours before he would pause to think of something else to talk about. Then the other person would cut in and start talking. We typically would go back and forth for five or six hours and then bust out laughing. Then we would stop. We practiced that technique about twice a week to build up my conversation until I got pretty good at talking while switching topics.

Another popular system we had used was writing <u>scripts</u>. We would write down an imaginary conversation on paper with an imaginary woman. We wrote down our introductory line (Hello pretty lady how are you doing?), and then we wrote down what we anticipated her to say (I'm doing fine). The next line we wrote would be: can I walk that way with you? Then we would write down the anticipated response: (Yes). We kept writing what we felt would be said by us next and then the young ladies response. Then we wrote our reply again, and then her response again. We would continue writing up to about eighteen to twenty pages until we felt confident enough to try out these anticipated conversations for real when we hung out on the corners.

I will not talk about other systems I used because I want to get to the point of what I've been trying to say up to this stage. The pimp books and movies I read and seen-do not cover every detail of young persons early years on the streets. Those books don't talk about all he went through year after year with drugs, alcohol, and crime. They skip too many events before he got that stable of women with the big car, fat bankroll, and fancy clothes. The common systems that are used for the

The Mack

development of players are not even talked about. What about the teenage wannabes that ends up dead or doing life in the penitentiary? Those pimp books and movies are put on the market to sell and not to educate. It's all about the big bucks. One of the main purposes of this book is to educate our young people (and those who have been in the game) to the realities of street life. There is an eventual goal and success that is never talked about in books or the movies.

There is supposed to be a happy ending to all the mess that a street hustler goes through. I am continuously witnessing young and old players coming off the streets, giving up drugs and alcohol, while their broken lives were being rejuvenated, but many of them still don't know what to do next.

The many friends that I grew up with as teenagers-never talked about the happy ending. We never talked about the mansion, multiple fancy cars, the multi-millions of dollars saved up, independent contracting jobs, entrepreneur businesses, a college degree, and self-education. We were ego tripping and just elated to have a few ladies putting money in our pockets. We had one car each and one place to stay. We didn't work for anyone. We relied on the cash from our women and other street games that were implemented periodically. We thought we were living the American dream. Drugs and alcohol dominated our pastime, along with hanging out in the pool halls, discos, and on the street corners flagging down ladies for their phone numbers. We were young mack's living for the moment on a daily basis. Nobody cared about saving money. We spent money as fast as it came. It was something we needed and there was never enough. Drugs and alcohol was our next necessity. We could no longer function without it.

I would eventually hear about one of my buddies getting shot and killed. Some died from overdoses, others got big time in the penitentiary, and many of them are still strung out on drugs with no savings or ambitions. Tragedy came with the turf. That was not the ending we expected. As a matter of fact, nobody cared about the ending. We were hustling well and lived for the moment. I hope to help many hustlers with this book by continuing to explain the different styles of players. I want them to have the choices that I and many other hustlers didn't have during our younger years. Even those who choose not to call themselves players, have issues to deal with. I discuss that in the <u>Female Non Player</u> and <u>Male Non Player chapters</u>. I will continue to provide all the information needed

The Epitome of a Player

to bring about that happy ending for many young people. Then it will be up to them to decide if this book can help them.

The word mack is a street slang that's addressed to a man who has a gift of being able to converse with a person better than any other player in the game. It is realistic for me to say that a typical mack eventually chooses to use his gift of persuasive assertiveness to charm the ladies into serving his every need and desire.

I'm going back into time before my friends and I started talking about having plenty of money, fancy cars, nice clothes, jewelry; going to parties, lunches, dinners; buying gifts, and romancing. We didn't know about the forms of admirable living that is accredited to the money given to a player by his women. Nor did we understand the ideas that he had to create and implement on his own with the exchange of ideas between other players and hustlers in the game.

There is this scenario of young, hip, people, around the age of sixteen going to parties that's given in their parent's living room, dining room or basement. Sometimes all three areas are used at the same time. They do their fancy steps and turns on the stepping music. And of course they get a little feel for a thrill during the slow dancing. It is very typical to have some beer, wine, hard liquor and marijuana at the parties. For those parents who made sure there was no drinking or marijuana smoking, the teenagers simply drank and got high before coming. The young men would give cans of beer to the ladies to put in their pocket books so they could smuggle it in the party. For the most part the parties went very well. Sometimes one person would get too drunk and high, act a little wild, and depending on the neighborhood; a party would get shot out sometimes. But the incidents like that was seldom a problem in the 1960's and early 1970's.

On days when there was spare time-the teenagers would practice their dance steps in their parents' homes. It was also typical of the young men to stand on the street corners and talk to the pretty young ladies as they walked by. That caught me by surprise because I had never heard of anyone doing that. My friends would tell me what to say, how to say it, and when to say the appropriate words to a young lady to get her to stop, let me socialize with her, and get her phone number.

This turned into a sort of fun game. We made an agreement to try and get at least five phone numbers from five different women every time we hung out on the corners to rap to the ladies. We felt that if we obtained at least five phone numbers then we could take out for those women who would give us the wrong number, and those conversations that don't go well over the phone. That technique would typically guarantee us at least one or two good phone numbers (where as the conversation came out ok over the phone and we agreed to talk again at a future date).

After getting good with our conversation we decided that all of us were professionals, and because of that, we should be able to get a phone number from the young ladies wherever we were at. It could happen in a store, the park, the Laundromat, in school, on the bus, the subway train, in church, at a party....

Every now and then we would gather together inside our parent's basements or in the alley, and talk about the responses we were getting from the ladies-while drinking booze and smoking marijuana. We would discuss the lines that worked-along with any corrections and adjustments necessary to make our conversations better. We would also go over our scripts together every now and then. But it was still our responsibility to write our own scripts on our own time when we had a chance.

We were smooth; and we did not run up to women grabbing their hand or trying to force a conversation with them. Acting frantic was not our profile. We were very polite, very respectful, and professional gents. This sad circumstance of young men forcing conversations with women should stop because it's bad for the game.

We got hooked on booze and stuck on cool. Eventually we were doing well enough financially to buy marijuana and harder drugs. There was no mention about what to do if we got hooked on drugs, alcohol, and cigarettes. Nobody expected to get a habit on anything.

Having multiple women, sex, money, narcotics, and no future, became our make up. There was no veteran in the game to help us out. I don't know what persons my young peers learned from, but I learned enough from them to organize a family of women to hustle with. I also got hooked on all the bad habits that come with street life. I discussed that area of my life during my teenage years in order to identify with those young people in many neighborhoods that are coming up the same way my friends and I came up.

This book is about helping young players make better choices in life; this can help them avoid the penitentiaries and graveyards. It is appropriate to think about why you're hanging out on the streets, and why

The Epitome of a Player

you're using drugs, alcohol and cigarettes. Where has it got you in life so far?

By the time a young man reaches eighteen years of age it is time to think about going to college or taking up a trade or going to the military. It is time to start thinking about moving out of your parent's home and establishing a mature and responsible lifestyle. Your parent's should not have to take care of you once you reach eighteen because you are able to work a full time job and take care of yourself. Even if you go to college you can still work full time. Many teenagers choose to stay at home while going to college, but they still work and prepare for life on their own after college.

I went to college at the age of eighteen and then I went to the military. I didn't stick with either one of them long. When I got out of the military I got a job, a car, and my own place to stay. My other friends got their own places to stay also, but the lifestyle of drugs and no career objectives got a lot of them killed or shot up.

Those young men on the streets right now that's involved with women, prostitution, macking and drugs, (while living with their parent's) should think about why they are still living with a parent and not in a college dormitory.

They need to decide if a parent or friend will be able to get them out of jail if they get caught selling drugs or pandering. They should also think about why someone else should have to come up with money to get them out of jail because of an ill advised decision to do something illegal. They knew that they were doing wrong in the first place.

Young hustler's should stop thinking that someone else is suppose to come up with money to help them out when they intentionally do all the wrong things in life. They should not be living with parents while doing drugs and pandering. They should be able to pay their own way out of jail (or stay in there if they can't), and not depend on relatives or anyone else to foot the bill. They should pay for their own mistakes and then decide how long they can continue paying attorneys for handling their cases.

A young person reading those pimp books and watching those types of movies can easily be disillusioned into thinking that all you need is a decent conversation to be on your way. By the time I was twenty-one years of age all my friends including myself had started doing hard drugs.

I had three women during that time. Some of my other friends had several women of their own. We were young mack's making money, but there were several problems no one thought about or cared about. What in the heck was our destination? Where were our business plans, our savings, and our goals?

Everything started out as something cool to do. We were standing on street corners talking to ladies, practicing our dance steps, smoking a little marijuana, and drinking a little beer. That turned out to be a lifestyle. And in actuality, those were our goals whether we realized it or not. We go to work; and then hang out after work to do drugs and go to parties. We had fun doing those things during our teenage years and wanted to keep on having fun doing them when we were adults.

Those young people who are macks should ask themselves these following questions and have a mature responsible answer.

1. Do you have money saved up to get yourself out of jail instead of calling someone else up for help?

2. Are you living in your own apartment or house (and not with a parent)?

3. Are you currently using drugs, alcohol, and cigarettes? If so, do you have a system for getting off them if you get a habit? You have a very high risk of losing your life in some form or fashion because of the use of those illicit substances.

4. Are you spending money to buy your kids clothes and food? Do you take them out to different activities like the zoo, children's parties, the museum, the circus, and other events?

5. If you don't have kids and are active sexually with one or more women; are you prepared to support your kids financially if you have any?

6. Do you think it's ok to beat a woman if you consider yourself to be a mack? If so, you are wrong because the style of the mack and beating women has long played out. It is an old outdated system. Women are not cats and dogs that you beat on. They are human beings with feelings just like you.

The Epitome of a Player

7. Has anyone ever introduced you to the style of the <u>man of leisure</u> and <u>gentleman of leisure</u>? They don't use drugs or alcohol, and don't do any illegal activities. Those two styles have been around for a while, but many young people don't know about them.

8. Do you feel it is ok to take the life of another person? The misuse of guns has taken many lives needlessly. You are not the creator of life, so you are not the one to decide if someone should die because of your ill feelings towards that person. Be responsible and respect the lives of other people. Don't use any guns and discourage your friends from using them.

9. Do you have a career in mind that provides a positive direction in life, such as a real estate investor, an independent contractor or entrepreneur? Many young hustlers don't like working for others and that's one of the reasons why they turn to crime. Try staying in school and learning a legitimate business that you can be your own boss in.

10. Is it difficult for you to make adjustments and accept change? I am giving young people all the right reasons to leave the streets alone and then accept responsibility in life by making mature decisions. Change isn't easy but change is a part of life that will always be there. A positive change should be appreciated. Young people should learn to be adaptable in their lives and always make the appropriate adjustments in life whenever it's necessary. If you are hanging out on the streets and doing all the wrong things for all the wrong reasons then pull off the streets. Hurry up to register in school and establish a respectable career working for yourself or a good job working for someone else. Some young men don't really mind working for someone else if the job is very flexible and they're making pretty good money. There's nothing wrong with that either.

Many people think that a mack is someone who is a panderer with several women prostituting, playing credit cards, boosting (stealing), playing checks, burglarizing; robbing, and doing anything to get money and bring it to the player. A mack is someone who is simply better with

The Mack

his conversation than any other player in the game; and that doesn't mean he has to choose pandering as his source of income. Many macks will change their style to a con man. Some of them will leave the streets alone to become a salesman, a politician, an attorney or a preacher.

Now I am going back to the basics again. This time I'm going to go back a little farther than my days of stepping, hanging out on corners, getting phone numbers from ladies, and having three to five girl friends at a time. I am going back to the time when I was fourteen years of age before my mother moved on the Southeast side of Chicago (where my lifestyle got much faster).

I was standing by Ogden Park around 63rd and Racine Street in Chicago-talking to three of my friends the same age and one of them was talking about a young man who was living with his mother. He had three women bringing him money. They made money any kind of way they could get it. He was considered to be a mack. That was the first time the thought had crossed my mind about living a lifestyle like that, because it sounded pretty cool, intriguing, and very stylish to be acknowledged as someone who could handle women in that fashion.

There is an old saying on the streets that <u>the thought is the cause of it all</u>. It was not my intent to entertain the thought. I unexpectedly allowed myself to do just that at the age of sixteen. I ran into all kinds of problems with jail time, drugs, fights, and unwise arguments. The lifestyle wasn't as glamorous as those pimp books and pimp movies made it look. It wasn't even as cool as my friends made it sound.

I told that true story to identify with young people who have gotten caught up with the same thought I got caught up in when I was fourteen years old. Our young people of today have gotten truly mesmerized with egotism, style, coolness, and having multiple women. Men strive off intrigue and challenges. Young men like the good feeling they get when their friends tell them how cool and down in the game they are with the fancy cars, nice jewelry, nice clothes and attractive women.

Well, many of those women don't look very attractive several years later behind the use of excessive drugs, alcohol, ten million dates and smelly breath from liquor and cigarette smoke. The players don't look so cool for the same reasons; and after spending many days and years behind bars; all his money and cars are gone from drug addition. At that point, the only woman he can get is one who will go half on a bag of dope with him. She will eventually vanish when the drugs vanish. That's a reality when men can't come up with money quick enough to feed a woman's drug habit (and in actuality, the drugs are her man, not you).

Now I will go back to that same incident when I was fourteen years old while hanging out at the park with my friends. This time I will hypothetically talk about a veteran in the game that comes along and hear us talking. He decides to explain the four popular styles of players (pimp, mack, man of leisure, and gentleman of leisure). He talks about having a necessary balance in our daily lives (25% physically, 25% mentally, 25% emotionally, 25% spiritually) in order to have peace, stability, maturity and wisdom in all that we do. The veteran would have made a good point. Young people will listen to someone who can explain circumstances to them in a mature, respectful, and understanding manner (the game is about respect).

Many parents have a tendency to be a little too harsh on their children when they discover that their kids are engaging in drug use and early teen sex. We parents were not perfect as kids and we will never have perfect children. Undue harshness has never been an appropriate system for educating children on the proper, respectful, and sophisticated aspects of mature growth doing their teens.

Many parents used drugs, alcohol, and cigarettes, while growing up; so it is pertinent that they humble themselves and be a friend to their kids. Try showing some understanding about how they got caught up in narcotics. Apply loving advice and support to provide and explain a better way of living. And I mean that they be the kind of friend their kids can come to and talk about anything without their parents getting upset.

Many children want to talk to their parents about drugs, alcohol, and early teen sex, but are afraid their parents will get upset if they confide their inner secrets with them. I am not saying that this process is easy for parents, because it was not easy for my son's mother and I, to talk to our son Ernest Ivy III about drugs, alcohol, cigarettes, and early teen sex. I became a friend to my son; and because of that, he has been and still is able to talk to me about anything, no matter what it is. His mother and I realized that friendship is part of parenthood and nobody said the process had to be easy.

The rewards are very gratifying when our kids grow up drug free with a good education and a balanced lifestyle with marriage included. Our good example as parents will help them be good examples of parents to their children, because they will imitate the style we used on them. Of course the parents who are using drugs and alcohol will have to give them up before talking to their children about giving them up. It has to be obvious that they will not understand how you can ask them to stop doing something that you as the parents are actively doing.

Many parents don't seem to realize that we need to give up _all_ of the erroneous activities. We don't want to pass our mistakes onto our children. We brought our children in this world and no one asked to be here. We owe it to them and ourselves to be responsible parents by raising them in a drug free environment with the explanation of how scruples apply in their lives.

I certainly would have chosen the man of leisure or gentleman of leisure style. That caliber of a player has high intellect and doesn't get high off drugs or drink alcohol. Many of them don't smoke cigarettes. That invaluable information was not available to me at a young age. Up until the writing of this book, it has not been available to many young people all over the world.

I am going to list a ten-step program for young people to think about implementing in their lives so that they can have goals, direction and purpose in life. I would also like to acknowledge that young people don't have to put a title on them at all as a pimp, mack, gentleman of leisure, man of leisure or lady of leisure. You can simply classify yourself as a businessperson who is trying to make it in life just like anybody else who didn't ask to be here. I am going over those different styles for the benefit of those who are already on the streets hustling, and for those who are thinking about stepping out there.

It is merely necessary to understand your surroundings and make wise choices in life. Now think about the following ten steps for making any necessary adjustments to elevate your game. This will help you be the player you was meant to be or simply the businessperson you was meant to be. Either one is fine so long as you're legal and taking care of yourself.

1. If you are using drugs, alcohol and cigarettes; go to a treatment facility to get help getting off them. You were simply misled and misunderstood the appropriate norms of survival and peace in life. You will need a clear head in order to set positive goals and follow them. You will also extend your chances of living longer by keeping those items out of your system. Following this step will

The Epitome of a Player

make you a positive role model for young people, as well as your own kids who will love you for it.

2. Go back to school and get your G.E.D. or high school diploma. This will help balance your life out emotionally, because you will feel very good about yourself and about the accomplishment.

3. Think about getting some college; whether it is one, two, three, or four years. You can even think about six years of college for a master's degree. Some of you may prefer going to a trade school after high school and that's ok too; but always keep some college in mind. The more education you get the better. Education should never cease in ones life no matter how old you get. If you don't continue to exercise your mind you could lose it, so why waste it? Education is knowledge and knowledge is game.

4. Think about learning a second language like Spanish or French. You will definitely look more bonafide as a player if you can speak more than one language, and there are more job opportunities for people who speak more than one language.

5. Open up a bank account. Many young people blow their money on drugs, alcohol and cigarettes. Then when they take a bust and go to jail, they have to call up a friend or relative to get them out. In many cases the friend or relative don't have the money, so they have to sit in jail a long time; then settle for a public defender that is going to get paid whether he does a good job or not. This means the young player will possibly have to do a little time in the penitentiary. If he doesn't have any savings or anybody to put money on the books for him, he will have to struggle; and believe it or not, there are convicts doing time who have bank accounts with a lot of money in it. They were smart enough to have savings before they took a bust.

6. Make a decision on what type of career you want. You could be a real estate broker, a real estate investor, a stockbroker; a singer, a football player, basketball player, soccer player, or entrepreneur. There is big money in all those careers. You will be in control of

The Mack

managing your own time without working for someone else unless you choose to do so. Remember, a gentleman of leisure does things at his own pace when he gets ready. You will need to pick out a career that allows you to do just that. Like I said earlier in this book, hustlers don't like working for other people so make a strong effort to get plenty of education under your belt and go about the game proper.

7. Try to find a mentor. A mentor is a wise and trusted teacher, and a good counselor. Find someone who is doing well in life that you look up to and admire. Ask that person for advice on setting goals. This idea is very important for the young hustlers who came from broken up homes; where as one or both of the parents are missing. Humble yourself and ask someone for help. There are plenty of people who are willing to reach out and help. Just try it. My peers and I didn't acknowledge anything about a mentor when we were teenagers so take advantage of this advice.

8. Start an exercise program. Your body is a gift and a gift should be well taken care of. This will be good for your physical, mental, and emotional growth. Your bones will get weak when you get older, so weightlifting will help keep them very strong. Calisthenics and joggings are very good for cardio (the heart) strength training and endurance. A high-quality exercise program will keep you relaxed and mentally alert. You will appreciate the effort and rewards in the short and long term stages of your life. I periodically hear of someone passing out after jogging up one flight of stairs. That's a dog gone shame. An exercise program will help a man's sex life, because women will get disappointed when a man only last a few seconds in bed; then lay there like a corpse because he's burned out. Come on man, don't' embarrass men. Be a stud, get yourself in shape and give her the ride of her life you dog gone lover you!

9. There are too many young people walking around talking about <u>I got to find myself</u>. Would you all give me a cotton picking, dog gone break! How long do you have to be on this Earth before you understand that you're a human being? Isn't that simple? Don't degrade yourself and don't rank the game by not having spiritual

The Epitome of a Player

balance. Talk to somebody who you believe can be mature and respectful while bringing you back to the real world, and yes, you blew it. Ask that person if you can borrow one of his/her books in that area. The last thing a player needs to do is get a pleasant relationship with a nice young lady and then she realizes you're trying to find yourself. Don't rank yourself with the dumb stuff.

10. Don't procrastinate! Start working on these ten concepts right now. This game is not for the slow; it's for the swift, the strong and most of all, for those who can endure.

I have plainly laid out the foundation for the groundwork to be done. Only you can build up your own image by taking advantage of the ideas and suggestions in this book. As you read these chapters you will notice that I repeat certain details. That's because redundancy (repetition) sinks into a person's mind and stay there.

I want the concepts in this book to sit and register in young people's minds all over the world. I am presenting a realistic approach to a player's game. This effective decision-making will provide stability and independent living in your lives. Don't guess what this game is all about and don't guess your way through life. If you have any doubts about anything I discuss in this book then ask someone you respect as being knowledgeable in this fast pace game for clarification. It's ok to do that.

Just don't guess at what you're doing, because your life depends on it. The overcrowded jail cells and penitentiaries are proof that many people needed this book or a better system (if they had a system at all), than what they had in order to justify what they were doing. It would have helped them go about their business more appropriately with very little repercussions.

6

THE PIMP

The word pimp is equated to the term panderer. According to Webster's II New Riverside University Dictionary: a panderer is a go between or liaison in sexual intrigues. The second definition states that a panderer caters to the base desires and the tastes of others or exploits their weaknesses.

I will agree with the first definition and I agree with the second definition about a pimp catering to the base desires and tastes of women. But I don't believe the third one is popular (he will exploit the weaknesses of women) because typically, he could care less about whether a woman decides to be a part of his family (unless he's a weak player).

A pimp has the meanest and coldest human nature than any of the players I have just described. He doesn't care if a woman is fine as wine. She either wants to be about the things he's about or she doesn't.

He no doubt acts as a liaison in sexual intrigues. But he wouldn't blink an eye or lose one minute of sleep if a woman does not choose to become a part of his family. They serve his every need and desires out of choice and desire. He is not on a sympathy mission for the weak at heart. He doesn't have a heart. He took his heart out and threw it away because there is no room for lullabies and heart felt feelings in this player's lifestyle. As a matter of fact, it's not easy for a woman to be a part of the pimp's life; because he looks for the fastest and toughest women in the game. She will have to go through a qualifying session in order to meet his approval. A woman can't just take it upon herself to choose the pimp. He will let her know that her interest is fine, but he has to choose after she does. Then it will be up to him to decide if she will be allowed in his family. It is a privilege, because the player's family is the epitome of his world.

A woman can express her desire to be a part of his life (if he likes what he sees). He will let her know that he has to go out with her and talk to her on the phone every now and then in order to get to know her better (it's called the interview). And that's exactly what he does. They go out to dinner, to the movies, plays, parties, and whatever else they decide on. Sometimes a woman is chosen right on the spot if her game and make-up (looks) is really down like that (I've experienced it several times); but in

The Epitome of a Player

that scenario, she is typically introduced to the player by one of the ladies in his family (she's halfway there at that point).

The pimp is too smart to think that he is taking advantage of a woman who has a desire to be with him. He will know that the average woman has read some pimp books, seen some pimp movies, and have had conversations with her girlfriends about players. That's why their interest was built up for that type of man before they even ran into him.

Only a novice in the game would actually think that he <u>turned her out and made her a part of his family</u> (get real). She will be laughing to herself once she realizes he's thinking that way, and acknowledge him as a novice; which means she will not be with him for a long time. Sport'n ladies are looking for professionals who have an established reputation on the streets. They will stay with a novice long enough to enjoy him sexually (if he is attractive to them) then they choose a veteran pimp as soon as they can't stand the novice anymore.

Many women choose to be with a pimp because that's the type of man who will definitely whack her a few times if she gets out of line. She believes that's what she truly deserves every now and then for being the ruthless and scandalous person that she is. She doesn't want a man who will let her have her way with him. She wants a man who will speak up. He has to be tough in dealing with hardships and the climb of success in life.

In other words, she wants to make sure that she doesn't end up with a mama's boy. Many women have changed their own babies' diapers. They don't want to change the diapers of grown men who whine and need a pacifier in their mouth when things get tough in life.

Many women will become a part of the pimp's family and purposely start disputes with the other women, hoping to run them off. When all of them are gone she will pressure the player into marrying her. Many players do marry one of their women because it is difficult to find a woman who understands him and his need for a fast and daring life. She knows he has the ability to work independently for himself at whatever occupation he chooses if he leave the game. She already knows he is going to scare many of his women off anyway; with his temper or physical abuse. All she will have to do is endure, persevere, and wait for the right situation and timing to catch him in the appropriate mood. Then she will talk about their future and the wedding bells. It normally happens when

The Pimp

the pimp has lost all his women, money, property, and is ready for a change.

I have just talked about a fantasy (marriage) that doesn't come easy for a woman because the pimp is true to the streets. He is not quick to go and get a 9 to 5 job like the other players (mack, man of leisure, and gentleman of leisure) if times get tough, and they get short on money. A pimp is the only player who will turn a date with another man or woman if he loses the women in his family. In many cases the pimp will keep turning dates with others if his money stays short and he want drugs to get high on.

The pimp is a true survivor of the street game. There are many people that think he is a homosexual. That's true for some of them, but not all of them. Many of them still prefer a woman to a man when it comes down to a serious relationship. They simply live up to their reputation of turning a date when times get tough; they're backed up in a corner, and need to survive. They don't place limitations on themselves like the other players. They go all the way and it would take more than a pack of wild horses to pull them off the streets. They are there to stay unless their life is at stake if they don't make a change (and many don't change).

The over indulgence with drugs and alcohol have brought many players (including the pimp) off the streets into drug treatment centers. Many hustlers are realizing that they were prepared for anything and everything except for a drug habit. They simply didn't expect it to happen. When things change, the player's should change (at least the wise ones).

There were quite a few days when someone would approach me and say, what's happening pimp? And I would correct them and say: "I'm not a pimp." Then I'd tell them what my style was at that time. Eventually I realized that the term pimp (when someone uses it as a casual hello) is also used as a greeting from one player to another. This statement is an acknowledgement that they're both about the same thing, even if their styles are a little different.

In other words, just because somebody says hey pimp what's up, doesn't mean you practice that style or that's your title. The word (pimp) is often times, used periodically, as a greeting and acknowledgement for those who play street games, con games, or whatever their hustle may be. If you are seen on the set a lot, then someone may use that greeting with you. Don't panic and don't freak out. Hustlers know what your style is and

The Epitome of a Player

they are not tagging a name on you. Simply relax, be smooth, and accept the game for what it is.

As the years went by, and after I got out of the penitentiary in January of 1981, I realized that many hustlers did not know the difference in the styles of players. A lot of them had never heard of a man of leisure or gentleman of leisure. I considered that to be a dog gone shame because it makes all the sense in the world to do your homework so that you will know what the heck you're talking about on those streets. I have had some players say to me: would you go over those different styles again? I basically got tired of going over and over the same thing, so I decided to include those styles in this book. One of the biggest atrocities in the game is for someone to question a young player on what the different styles of players are, and he or she is not able to explain it.

It is of the utmost importance to look like a professional player, talk like one, and carry yourself like one. Everything about your make up has to dictate that you're qualified, certified, and know what the heck you're doing while in the mix. If you are confused and have some doubts about where you're headed in life, and why you're out there on those streets; then you are really just having fun getting high on drugs and taking a shower in sex. It would be a good idea to think about that, because many hustlers and those poor excuses for players, should realize-there's supposed to be a darn happy ending (rather than broke and full of cum) to being <u>in the fast life</u>. That's right! I said there should be a happy ending to all the mess you put yourself through on the streets.

You didn't exactly pack a lunch bag and go on a field trip when you decided to endeavor in street game. Make something out of the mess and then pull out of it with something worthwhile, like your life. And who knows, if you haven't messed up too bad; a house, car, clothes, jewelry, and some cash-could be part of your new make up. Don't leave the streets with not even a bone to chew on; cus if you do; nobody's going to throw you a bone (you get what your hand calls for). This book is about getting hustlers back on the right track (so they can live one more hour), and giving them some wise decisions to make before they step into the game, whether it's on or off the streets.

The pimp and mack have similarities in their style of living. Both of them utilize women and their services for financial gain. And both of them prefer street hustle as opposed to working a 9 to 5 job. The only difference is that a mack will not turn a date if things get tough. He will

The Pimp

work a job first, but being true to the game, he will only keep the job for three to five months (if that long). He will work long enough to get his money and women back in order, and then he's gone from that job. Such is life.

The man of leisure and gentleman of leisure may not even start out on the streets. They may never use drugs at all. Their style is an entirely different program. It's a world that many hustlers did not know existed. But those styles are rapidly taking the place of the outdated pimp and mack style.

There are many pimps and macks switching over to the man of leisure and gentleman of leisure style. That's because they have extended knowledge and experience in the game. Those who were using drugs and alcohol are dropping them like flies or like a ball of fire were in their hands. Many players knew that they were living in a fast game, where as you get your money and pull out or you pull out with your knowledge and use it to acquire money. But they got stuck on drugs, sex, and parties. That is a mistake that cost many players their life or their freedom. They ended up doing a lot of time or life in the penitentiary.

Everything about the street life and hustle is not found in books or acknowledged by every hustler. There is a common sense policy that goes without saying when you are in the mix. What I mean by that is; if you can't stop continuously putting illicit narcotics in your body day after day, and year after year, and do not expect any negative repercussions (like overdoses, heart disease, liver disease, lung disease, cancer or whatever), then you have made an unrealistic approach to the game, drugs, alcohol; and cigarettes. Common sense is not part of your intellect in those regards.

I will use an example of eating only pork day after day. At some point and time you will start to look like a pig. The bad cholesterol will start clogging up in your arteries and cause a heart attack or high blood pressure.

Cigarettes have been the cause of many deaths and illnesses. But many people still smoke them day after day, year after year, as if nothing negative will happen. A lot of them hear about the person who smoked for sixty years and nothing happened. Well how many people got that lucky? That's like the street hustler hearing about the player who got shot 8 times, stabbed 7 times, been in the penitentiary 5 times, have almost overdosed on drugs 7 times, and is still living. Well how many stories do you hear

The Epitome of a Player

like that? Do you really feel that those odds are in your favor for receiving that kind of miracle?

It's really not a good idea to try and live off somebody else's miracle. When people gamble at the horse races and casinos, they play for the best odds. Not many people play for the long shot. When people fill the lines up in front of stores, gas stations, and wherever lottery tickets are sold, for a chance to try and win those 150,000,000 dollars or more, they realize that only one person out of millions is going to win.

The same thing applies to street life. Only one person out of millions will get stabbed and shot multiple times, and then spend many years in the penitentiary; possibly overdose on drugs numerous times, while fortunate to live and talk about it. The only reason that person was fortunate enough to live is so that he can tell others how insane a lifestyle of drugs, alcohol, and the streets are. Their testimony will help give many people the opportunity to make better decisions with their lives.

The fine art of adjusting to and appreciating change has to be exercised in order to be successful in the game. The styles of the pimp and mack have consisted of drugs, alcohol, and the brutality of their women. That was going on many years before I was born January 19, 1953 (oops, I'm telling my age).

Many players have found those styles to be exhausting, frustrating, and a sweat to their style. In other words, the money isn't worth it if a player has to beat his woman to act right and make money. And it's not worth the headache of dealing with the ladies mood swings that comes with a drug habit. Not to mention the money spent getting the ladies out of jail periodically, and then getting himself out of jail periodically; paying attorneys, looking out for the stick up man, and fighting (or killing) male dates who give your women a hard time.

You will be constantly relocating because the police are watching your house. And what if one of your women overdoses or get killed by a trick? You are simply helping to destroy lives and you are susceptible to catching periodic diseases passed on by one or more of your women (it's inevitable).

The man of leisure and gentleman of leisure make their own money. They are free of drugs and alcohol use. Many of them don't smoke cigarettes either. That is a more relaxed lifestyle with one woman in their corner. In many cases (with the gentleman of leisure) she is his wife. As a matter of fact, they usually make much more money than they would if

The Pimp

they choose the pimp and mack style, which is all show and flash, and the struggles are not worth it.

This is the conclusion of the four different styles for young male players. Now I am about to discuss the same concern about the female player in the next intense chapter titled: <u>The Lady of Leisure</u>.

7

THE LADY OF LEISURE

Scripture states: (proverbs 5:3-6) the lips of an immoral woman drip honey, and her mouth is smoother than oil: but in the end she is bitter as wormwood, sharp as a two-edged sword. Her feet go down to death; her steps lay hold of hell. Lest you ponder her path of life-her ways are unstable: you do not know them.

She is a cold hearted, blunt, female player. A spiritual balance will be necessary in a man's life to focus and understand the woman whom he is engaging in a conversation with. He needs to know exactly what his/her intentions are. I have spoken about the importance of you having a balance in this life (mentally, physically, emotionally, and spiritually). I was not trying to put that lightly; I was serious.

Many men believe that they can hit it off with any woman they encounter and that's a big mistake. It has got to register in a man's mind there are many women who were born before them, been out in this cold world before them, and therefore have more experience in the game than them. But it's hard to explain that to many big headed men who think they are Gods gift to women and Einstein on top of it.

The lady of leisure has been the downfall of many men whose ego made them believe they could play her, but got the game reversed on them. The men end up getting played. She is a professional; A master with the application of her lip-gloss, hair style, finger nails gleaming, and sexy outfits that show enough cleavage to attract a man's attention; even if he is on the other side of the street. She is a walking trap.

When I was sixteen years of age standing on the corner of 79th and Crandon on the East side of Chicago, one of my buddies was schooling me on what to say to a woman when she walk by, when to say it, and how to say it. He also told me that every person is not working the same program. For that reason, it was necessary to switch my conversation to leave her and then go to the next woman if the one that I was talking to was singing a different song than I was. Certain women could not figure out the real reason I was leaving. Sometimes they would look puzzled and that's ok, because socializing with women is a game of numbers.

You pick and you choose, pick and you choose, pick and you choose. You never just pick and take it from there because you can end up

The Lady of Leisure

with a big mess on your hands thinking you will work something out with a woman who is not about the program your on. Keep thinking like that and you won't last long in this game or in this life period. Many of these female player's have gotten many men shot, mugged, and killed for the sake of a buck or the sake of love. It's not that serious man. Those kinds of love get buried with you.

How about the incident when a man goes to a hotel with a sexy sporting lady (who is a street style lady of leisure and very unscrupulous), and he doesn't realize that she purposely leave the door unlocked so her pimp can come in while they are in bed and rob him? Sometimes the pimp shoots him to make sure there are no witnesses; or how about when a man goes in the alley with a sporting lady to turn a date and her pimp is waiting to rob him?

I might as well include the encounter with a young male player (new on the set) who engages a veteran female hustler in his corner and she ends up schooling him. Then he ends up serving her every need, to the point of robbery, theft or burglary. He hustles hard to come up with a way to bring money to her. She is a professional so don't be lame. Many male players leave the spiritual balance out of their life thinking that its square; but that is as far from the truth as you can get.

I will keep mentioning it in this book periodically until it sinks into the minds of many male players that game is knowledge of all types of information. There is no one category of knowledge that the professional male hustler can leave out of his vocabulary. Keep picking up many books on all subjects and never stop your learning. There is no stop date for taking in game, which is knowledge. It is endless learning progressions so learn to like it. As a matter of fact, learn to love it.

There are three different styles to the lady of leisure. One is found on the streets; the other is not on the streets and is single. The third one is not found on the streets and is married. I will discuss all three of them. It is imperative for unsuspecting men to think about what kind of relationship they are looking for with the women they pick up on the streets or off the streets, especially if he is the type who falls in love easily.

The one you pick up on the streets is only interested in money. You can get your feelings hurt and get ripped off for a nice piece of cash. The married man should be extra careful because she will break up a marriage if there's enough money involved. But men should not take it

The Epitome of a Player

personal. It's not personal. Everything and every man looks green to her (the color of money) no matter what race you may be.

If drugs are involved-you may get caught up in a sleazy scheme to harm another person for the sake of acquiring more money. The victim could easily be a relative that's related to her or the man. Neither party will care because both of them are getting high. Men should understand why they are out there and what to expect from street activity. The streets aren't a picnic area or amusement park.

The first female player I'm talking about is the street dweller. She may be part of a pimp or a macks family, or she may be outlawing (a sporting lady on the streets who don't belong in a player's family). She is typically addressed by several names (whore, prostitute, sporting lady, lady of leisure), but the term lady of leisure is the professional title for those women who have been on the streets for a few years and have gotten enough experience for a professional that understands the game; she know the ropes, and doesn't have to be out there.

The professional lady of leisure on the streets is there because she started using drugs again. She blew all her money or she is in the process of elevating her game off the streets. In either case she will not be on the streets long.

The female streetwalker entered the game the same as the male players did. She had gotten intrigued through the conversations with her girlfriends, read a book on street life, seen a few movies about the fast lane, or she got out there in order to make ends meet. She may have come from a broken family where one or both parents were not present. Many women are simply overly sensuous by nature and prefer to sell the sex rather than give it up for free.

Whatever the streetwalker's reason is for sexual solicitation; the thought is already on her mind when she runs into a player. A player was once called the <u>fancy man</u> a long time ago. He is fancy and professional with his words, clothes, and overall demeanor. At that point and time they go out together, get to know each other better; and then the compromise takes place. They typically choose to be as one and work together.

As I said before, it is ludicrous for a young inexperienced male player to believe he actually turned a woman out and put her on the streets. The thought and intrigue was planted in her mind long before she met him, so she was already curious about choosing. He simply presented the personality to her that she was inquisitive about. She more than likely

The Lady of Leisure

turned down advances from three or four players before she finally ran into the one who presented a conversation to her liking. It's almost time to choose at that point.

The thought of belonging to one man does cross the mind of the streetwalker occasionally. The question I am presenting to those ladies right now is: how much longer will you walk the streets before you settle down with one man? Many women knew that they were entering a fast game just like the men. You get your money fast and pull out, or you pull out with your knowledge and use it to acquire wealth. The overall pack of ladies on the streets are making the same old mistake that many young male players made by getting stuck on a feeling of drugs, sex, and false love.

Instead of going about the game the way it was presented (or should have been presented) they followed the examples of many others who ended up in the graveyards and penitentiaries. They either stayed on the streets too long or they got super high on some drugs one time too many; then went out and did something crazy that cost them time behind bars, or their life.

And the madness that goes along with what I just said; is that the same women (just like the men) continue to go back and forth to jail; and then back to the dope house. In other words, those who are constantly making the same old mistakes have vacated the real world a long time ago. They found a strange place in <u>outer space</u> where there is no such thing as responsibility, continued education, and having some structure in life (like homes, nice clothes, a car, and a decent income).

Many female streetwalkers have been away from their kid's much two long. The game was never meant to be that way. In order for the streetwalker to be <u>the epitome of a player</u> in this game, she has to realize that the fast lane of drugs, prostitution, and crime, was simply a phase of the game and not the final chapter. In other words, it is time to elevate to a professional level in the area of independent contractor, entrepreneur, or a prestigious position working for someone else (if you don't mind working for someone else).

This next lady of leisure has risen above the streets or never played the streets at all. She more or less will pick up a date here and a date there. It will be at bars, lounges, parties, grocery shopping, the Laundromat, the bowling alley, walking to the store or to a friend's house. Either way it goes, she has made a decision to organize a few (three or four) established dates that typically provide for her immediate needs; financially, mentally, physically, and even spiritually

She has become very well balanced but her spiritual knowledge is limited to the point that she is not ready for a one on one relationship. She is having too much fun and don't want to let go of that lifestyle. Why the heck should she? And that's her rationality. What can one man do for her anyway?

Drugs and alcohol is still predominant in her life. She is as close to the ultimate stage (which is the next lady of leisure) of the game as a female player can get. In order for her to be the epitome of a player in this cold fast lane, it would be highly beneficial for her to settle with just one man, and preferably, try marriage. Steady relationships with a man, on and off, usually, do not last long with her. She is too susceptible to adding numerous men to her list. Eventually she will be living in the past again.

As I said before, there is supposed to be a happy ending to all that you put yourself through on the streets. At some point and time there has to be an elevation of ethical character within your style, decision making, cleaning out your body; moving to a nicer neighborhood; then an elevated education should take precedence in your life. That phase should not be a problem, because many women think about other areas in their life to devote their time to while street hustling, or playing the field away from the streets with several men.

It is not too late. Go home, think it over, and make that change. Pick up the phone and call somebody you know who will give you sound advice and support. You simply needed to read about it in this book for the change to be your wake up call.

The third lady of leisure is the ultimate level of the game for a female player. Her life will be very well balanced (married or single) and absent of drugs and alcohol. The reason why I put emphasis on marriage is because it's an ultimate goal for many of them, but stability is still in their single life. She has either been on the streets or has never been out there. She has learned how to play the game of life by interacting with those in power positions who can be an asset to her career. She knows the ropes and the angles. She has gone back in school and has a self-taught reading program. She takes care of her kids, exercise, and goes out a lot with her husband whose life is well balanced also.

There are many women at this third and ultimate level who don't classify themselves as a professional lady of leisure. That's because many

The Lady of Leisure

people don't understand the term and may relate it to the street style, which is not the professional level. The only time a streetwalker should use the term lady of leisure is when she is in the process of rising above the streets and drugs. The word lady means: 1. A woman with the refined habits, along with gentle manners often associated with good culture and breeding. 2. A woman regarded as virtuous and proper.

It is inappropriate for a woman to specify her demeanor under the above two definitions while street walking and soliciting dates with the other beginners out there. Appropriate recognition and stature in the game has to be earned, and it comes with experience and knowledge. It is wise for the female novice on the streets (and those thinking about hitting the streets) to seek the advice of a female veteran who will lead them in the right direction and prepare them for professionalism in the fast lane. It is too dangerous to guess and the female streetwalker should get funeral and burial insurance? That's right; I said funeral and burial insurance! Do you think you're going to Santa's Village with a picnic basket when you hit the streets? It's not fair to your relatives if you expect them to constantly spend money to get you out of jail and try to come up with money to pay for your funeral and burial if you lose your life in that cold game you stepped into.

There are too many young men and women going in some room or vacant building getting high off drugs, and then coming up with some crazy notion that they want to be a player. Would you young people kindly give those dog gone drugs a rest long enough to think about what you're doing when you are sober and focused with a clear mind?

Many cities are running out of room in the graveyards and penitentiaries for the majority of you (who are green as grass) who stepped out there like a blind bat out of hell stuffing yourselves with any kind of drug that somebody put in front of you. The majority of street hustlers know I'm telling the truth. Someone could offer one of you a drug called <u>kick my butt</u> and you will say: "<u>hey, that sounds cool,</u>" and you will try it out. In other words, <u>say no to something</u>! Just because you got something that is not nailed down, doesn't mean you have to take it.

For too long, there has been a devastating misunderstanding of young people interpreting just what is street game and hustle? Well, you are not jumping on a merry-go-round or a swing and going <u>wheeeeeeee</u>. Hustlers are entering a deadly game of crime for fast money. These illegal practices on the streets should be avoid if possible; because there are other styles for players to practice that are not on the streets (which is for the lost and bewildered).

Just like the male player, the female player has to balance her life (spiritually, mentally, physically, and emotionally) for peace, contentment, and to also be competitive with other professionals. Many of you didn't step into the game you stepped into shame. And while I'm at it would you kindly put this book down and go to a friend or neighbor's house and take a bath? Then change that same shirt and pants you've been wearing for three months!

Somebody gave you that advice before you read it in this book, but you chose not to do it. You know who you are. I have been around too many streetwalkers who don't care about how bad they smell; and that scenario is clearly something out of the freaking darkness of doom! There are community programs that will help, so why stay stuck on that channel. Click the remote and find something better.

In order for the female streetwalker to be <u>the epitome of a player</u>, she will need to take her game off the streets and into the classrooms. Oh yeah, I said the classrooms. That's the very word many hustlers have been running from, because classrooms mean more education. Drugs kill and education don't. It's ok to live another hour or two.

Anybody can get high off some drugs and then hit the streets to jump in bed with a date for compensation. Those streetwalkers know they are getting about twenty or thirty dollars (if that much) for a date. And don't go telling that lie about you're getting fifty dollars or more because you won't be able to eat with so many lie bumps on your tongue.

You will get that price every blue moon; and that's because you lucked up and ran into a white-collar worker who simply felt sorry for you. And if he doesn't watch out, you will rip him off. That's right; you will rip him off; and your mother, father; brother or sister, for the sake of another godfather hit! Now tell me I'm lying so lightening can strike you down right now!

It doesn't matter how a woman ended up hustling on those streets. It was never necessary. There is a higher level than that in the game. You have to blend in with those professionals in colleges (and I don't mean pick up tricks in the schools) workshops, seminars, and investment groups, and on jobs, until you can establish your own legitimate business (which doesn't mean, become a madam).

The Lady of Leisure

The longer a woman sticks with the streets, the harder it will be for her to establish an honest and respectable relationship with an honest and respectable man. Personalities simply don't change overnight. This is a good time to make the change. Those who are strung out on drugs should contact a drug treatment facility because they will have mood alterations to deal with. Then try staying out of a relationship with a man for at least a year (unless you two were already together) because you will run the man away if he doesn't know you well.

It has been kept quiet that there was always suppose to be a happy ending from street hustle; and only you can make that happen. This is your fairytale and your storybook. You are still flipping the pages and you haven't got to the end yet. Forget the chapter you were on and start on a totally new chapter. You are your own audience. The stage is set and the show is not over until you are content with the ending.

8

THE FEMALE NON-PLAYER

I felt that the last chapter had a really happy ending. It was like a fairytale that started out a little crummy. All of a sudden there are all these blessings and some good fortunes that leave the person really elated and flabbergasted about her astounding new leaf on life, but many women don't consider themselves to be a player.

I decided to keep a good thing going by extending a woman's life after the streets-on into the marriage, or the significant other relationship (which doesn't really sound too cool). It wouldn't be fair for me to leave a woman hanging out on a limb after making an introduction to her rise to stardom in regards to a new fulfilling and rewarding lifestyle.

So the young lady has given up street life and has run into Mr. Everything; too smooth and too cool to be true? He has a mean lean as he walks. His words are so hip she would never give him any lip (maybe). At this point and time she has decided to put her past behind her and not even consider herself a player anymore. She really wants this relationship to work out and she's doing everything within her strong will power to be the woman of his sensational dreams. At that point, the couple gets married, go on the honeymoon, come back home, and their life is on the way. They live happily ever after. Yeah right! You know that sounded too darn good to be true.

I need to stop for a reality check. There is no need for me to continue trying to fancy the marriage up to this point and time. Located in the back section of many newspapers are numerous advertisements from attorneys that have offered their services in divorce cases. Those attorneys will even give you a free no cost consultation.

Now I'm really thinking, maybe I needed to take another look at that hook up? Here we have a fantastic relationship and now marriage, but as the couples decide to open up a newspaper, there are all these attorney advertisements on divorce. Now that's got to be a little discouraging, even if the sex is good (will it last?).

Do the attorneys know something that many people don't know? Attorneys that work all over the world will spend thousands of dollars ever year on advertisements for their services with divorce being high on their list. Well, let me see now, I think that I'm correct by saying that marriage counseling is not mandatory. That means anybody of legal age can go out and get a blood test, find two witnesses, a preacher; and say I do. The man doesn't even need to buy her a wedding ring. He can borrow one from somebody (like I did). Then he can return the ring after they say I do (like I did). They don't even have to go on a honeymoon if it's not affordable (there's always a bedroom close by). As a matter of fact-even if they are not of legal age to marry in one state-they can always go to a state where their age is legal and get married there.

If I had known all that when I was younger-I probably would have gone off to college to be an attorney. That way I could cash in on those divorce benefits. I wouldn't even need those ambulance chasers. I would do divorce cases only; then retire rich in several years.

So, as time goes by, the ultimate surprise has hit home with the newly wed woman who use to street hustle. She starts realizing that it's not easy learning how to treat a man like a human being over night. And that's the point I'm getting at in this chapter.

For quite a few years the streetwalker has turned dates with many men who meant nothing to her. If any sensual feelings of attachment came between her and a john (date), she would simply brush the feelings to the side. Everything about her life was based on money so she had to keep a cold heart with a business mind.

It is absolutely pertinent that the woman, who chooses not to call herself a player anymore, obtains marriage counseling. She also need to be patient for about a year before getting into a new relationship because she will experience mood swings after withdrawing off drugs and alcohol (the use of narcotics go along with street life). At this point she will have to think about men in an entirely different aspect. It will be necessary for her to find forgiveness for any man that she has a grudge against because she will unknowingly carry those ill feelings into the marriage.

I have run into women who are quick to make a decision to marry a man-even while they are active in their drug addition. That's a mistake. Even if the man doesn't use drugs the female player needs to deal with a reality check; which she will need a clear mind for. Why enter into a marriage with a man and then get him high before he can get you clean and sober?

A woman coming from a fast lifestyle was basically in control of the men in her life. Control was necessary in order to make sure that her money came out right. Now she's in a relationship where she has to give

The Epitome of a Player

up control in order to have a peaceful and respectable life. In actuality neither husband nor wife should be in control. The word control puts somebody in a robot state of mind. It can easily make someone think the other mates want his or her way, or there will be a verbal confrontation. The intent in marriage should be for the man and woman to have love, companionship, and the freedom to be the person they are. It will take an understanding of spiritual principles to appreciate humbleness and open mindedness to a new and special way of treating a person, and to a new way of living.

The ex-female player will need to forget all the pros and con's she used in her past street hustle so she will not play those unscrupulous mind games on her husband (or significant other). One of the main pro's and con's she may use is the torture of closing her legs and putting a lock on them so her other half can't have any sex, and he retaliates by treating her the same way at a later date. Then both of them are caught up in childish tick for tack. Give each other some coo-chi and stop treating each other like kids!

Her decision to hit the streets was not a mature and wise move. The maturity and wisdom has got to take place at some point and time. Learning how to make up after an argument is not easy, and it should be understood before the marriage that there will be some disputes every now and then. The balance (mentally, physically, spiritually, and emotionally) I am constantly bringing up has got to be put to good use for a respectable relationship. Getting a gym membership (or exercise equipment at home) will make a person feel good because exercise is a positive stimulation for the mind and body. It will be a plus if the gym has a whirlpool and steam room because those two commodities provide relaxation (along with the workout). The communication is a lot more pleasant in the marriage when couples are relaxed. You can always relax in a hot bath at home if the gym is minus a whirlpool and steam room.

Life can be very stressful at times and stress can cause friction between lovers, and this is where meditation can be helpful for emotional control. A good reading program will provide knowledge on controlling stress. If you obtain counseling services before and after marriage, you will add marvelous results to the relationship that you have.

Now I will talk about the woman who has never hustled on, or walked the streets soliciting dates. She has had several relationships with men that didn't work out. Now she has only one man, or should I say her

The Female Non Player

significant other (which doesn't sound like good security)? She never considered herself to be a female player and is just enjoying life to the fullest. One day she hopes to marry her man and live happily ever after.

Yeah, right! She no doubt has spent too much time talking to the Fairy God Mother. There's a possibility that she had, or may still have friends or relatives who hustled on the streets. Some of them are probably still on the set. I'm also sure that she has been in some of those football huddles women organize in the ladies room every now and then. Women don't hang out on street corners like men do. They hang out in groups in restaurants, schools, discos, lounges, or over one of their homes. If there are men around they will go to the ladies room as if it's a coincidence that they all had to powder their nose at the same time.

I have worked on a job for eighteen years and ten months in a department that had four women for every man. I was in many of those gatherings (or football huddles) when the ladies would socialize about men, sex, and money; with money being at the top of the list. When a man has worked with a large group of women for a while, the ladies don't care what they say around him because he becomes part of the gang.

What I'm expressing at this point is that the Ms. Goodie Two Shoe who didn't hustle or turn dates on the streets; has probably been in some of those conversations when women would get in their football huddles (in an office, the ladies room, or at lunch time while in the cafeteria), and then have their discussions about a man's money. They even discuss the tricks of the trade on how to squeeze those dollars out of him.

There had been a time when a man's looks alone would satisfy a woman, but inflation changed all that. There is an increasing competition of women displaying who can wear the nicer clothes, shoes, hats, coats, pocket books, scarfs, stockings, gym wear and lingerie

It is the belief of many women that a man should be prepared to buy some or many of those items (like I said, I have been in the middle of many of those football huddles). I started realizing that many women are looking for those gentlemen who keep themselves up mentally, physically, spiritually and emotionally. But making a nice buck is at the top of the list to satisfy their need to be financially secure.

A woman doesn't have to be exposed to street life in order to learn how to play the money game. The ladies football huddles are popular all over this world. They simply meet wherever they can in order to learn how to lay and play.

The Epitome of a Player

In other words, if a woman is telling me she is not a female player, but I know that her associates are players; and she keeps coming up with a periodic scheme to dig into my pockets or dig into other men's pockets; she will be guilty in my book of being a player by her associations and actions.

It will not be a good idea to take those tactics into a relationship with a man because they are player tactics and many women will take a man to be a darn Willie Lump-Lump. It doesn't make a difference whether he act like that or not. There is no respect coming from an unscrupulous woman who will want those dollars. Whatever the woman learned in those huddles that are devious, should be controlled or pushed out of her mind completely.

There was a time when a woman's looks meant everything to a man, but looks come second now. It doesn't matter if a woman is a model or look attractive enough to be one. Men are putting personality first (for those women who didn't know). This is a reality that started in the 1970's. Looks will attract but personality will keep him. Down to Earth women are high in demand now.

That viewpoint has become more and more pre-dominate over the years. Numerous men don't explain to women why they stopped calling. Men are seriously looking for honesty, humbleness, and sincere feelings from women. What difference does it make if a couple has a lot of money, but they can't get along half the time?

There is a little player in all of us, and that's because we have those inevitable associations with those who are slick, hip, and have been around the block a few times and back. It's ok if you choose to consider yourself a female non-player. Just drop the superficial game plans that were learned over the years. You will then have a better relationship with a man for that reason.

Now I am going to talk about the significant other relationship. That statement (significant other) is a growing phrase that took the place of the old school term, <u>this is my woman,</u> or <u>this is my lady</u>. Well, it's quite obvious that those old school terms have played out. Someone was sophisticated enough to come up with a term called <u>significant other,</u> or <u>my other half</u>.

Well ladies, I hope you don't mind if I help you out with the interpretation of <u>significant other</u> and <u>my other half</u>. You simply have a sex partner and nothing more. There is no guarantee that you two will get

The Female Non Player

married or stay together a long time-so it's not appropriate to let your feelings get too deep for the man because you are in an <u>open minded relationship</u>. In other words, anything can happen.

Just <u>hope for the best</u> and <u>prepare for the worst</u> (sorry). Many women have gotten hurt when those types of <u>other</u> relationships broke up. Those disappointments have led to distrust in future relationships.

The point I'm making by discussing several different relationships between a man and woman is for the sake of a woman being professional, down to earth, and honest with men; whether you tag a title of player on yourself or not. Don't let hurt feelings from previous relationships turn to hate. Avoid using crooked player characteristics because an affair with a man didn't work out.

Once a woman engages in intimate love with a man the two of you become a part of each other. Love is a strong motivator. Use it to do right with one another. There are men who will buy women gifts, take her on vacations, wine and dine her; and who knows what else; if he is financially able. But there will obviously be some occasional disputes and periodic misunderstandings because we won't find perfect people on Earth and it's good to acknowledge that.

Just respond with wisdom and tactfulness, because many men are not balanced spiritually and emotionally. Some men don't handle disputes very well and they will get physically abusive. Sometimes a woman says things very demeaning to a man (depending on what she has learned in the football huddles) because of a terrible misunderstanding, and that incident lead to physical abuse.

Even if the man had no intentions of being abusive it can happen if the woman is not careful enough. Always check to see if a man is living a balanced lifestyle (mentally, physically, spiritually, and emotionally). If he has no way of releasing tension (through exercising, the steam room and whirlpool), and has no values for spiritual concepts (which helps with humbleness), then a woman should seriously think twice before entering into a relationship with this man. But if she's already in one with this type of man, she should think twice about getting serious because there are too many men who feel they can handle life without an appropriate balance. If he does drugs or alcohol, you can add that to the list of warning signs about not getting serious with him. Many men consider drugs, alcohol, pills, cigarettes and sex, as a release for calming their nerves. Yes, they went out the door backwards.

The Epitome of a Player

A woman should be cautious about those assumptions; because typically when two people fall in love they want to be around each other a lot for companionship. They will also make love a lot; so make sure it's about love and not sex for the sake of calming nerves. There is a major difference between love and sex. Love means you feel good about each other even when sex is not involved. Sex means you want it just for the sake of doing it. A couple will benefit greatly when they're away from each other periodically enough to miss one another. That way love will have time to stimulate them to come together.

I mentioned earlier in this book that teenagers would benefit tremendously with the use of role playing in their class rooms (probably starting at the adolescent age of 11 or 12-on up to18 years of age) in order to help them get to an early start on how to respond appropriately in disputes with the opposite sex. This educational technique could help out tremendously in avoiding physical abuse when interacting with men. Otherwise, they will immediately learn from their peer groups and end up believing it's appropriate to give a man a piece of her mind rather than respond tactfully, assertively, and respectfully.

Maybe young and older adults could also benefit from such a program. The classes could be conducted in libraries, conference rooms, schools, churches, field houses or anyplace appropriately designated. I truly believe those programs will help couples to stop (especially men) killing one another in marital and significant other relationships. It sure won't hurt to make an effort to see how it works out. Otherwise, many parents will continue to lose their children to the graveyards from disputes that could have been handled more effectively.

The kids are the wave of the future. Adolescence on through their teenage years are very crucial, because that is the time frame when most of them will initiate learning about sex, crime, gangs; drugs, players and relationships. Many of the things they learn early in life will have a big impact on how they interact with each other in a one on one relationship between a young lady and a young man. This will be a lasting impression throughout their adult years.

If the kids don't learn about role-playing between their parents, relatives, and the school system, they will learn about it from the friends they hang out with on the streets. That has proven to be quite a disastrous nightmare in many cases. Women start learning at an early age-the games that their peers play, because they start those football huddles in the ladies room at an early age. It can be avoided with role-playing at an early age, and if not avoided completely, the female adolescence can learn what to retain and what to throw out of her mind.

It is important for women to realize that there is a relationship after the relationship. It will take humbleness and smoothness for her to be assertive, intelligent and tactful, whenever they talk after the break up. Especially if there are children involved; and the man is coming by to visit and take his kids out occasionally.

The woman should remember not to keep calling him rude names because of bitterness and hurt feeling on her part. That can only make him mad. Both of you had hurt feelings (not just one of you). He may then want to keep the kids out of spite or fight with her in front of the kids.

The relationship should be left alone when it's over. Take out some time and talk to a friend or counselor to help you get any ill feelings out of your mind. Meditate and picture yourself forgiving him while speaking maturely and respectful to him.

He needs to feel good about you as a woman after the relationship is over. Let him know that he is still special and you will appreciate him as a friend. But don't allow him to come visit you or make love to you after the break up unless you are sincerely thinking about getting back together with him. You should have a strong feeling that things will work out the next time around. It is also wise for the woman not to have another man sitting on the couch (for at least three months) right after the break up when he comes to see or pick up his kids (unless she feel another man is needed there for her protection).

There will still be some sentimental feelings on his part. Seeing another man over your place so soon after the break up may be taken as a sign of insensitive disrespect that can prompt anger (that he may not know how to handle), and ill feelings in his mind. That could prove out to be dangerous. It may even be wise for the woman to take the kids to see their father if she has a man living with her soon after the break up with her husband or significant other (until he get use to the thought of her having a new man in her life).

Women don't have to keep on filling up the battered women's shelters. They basically need to be conscious of the warning signs in a relationship or marriage. For instance, does he take a bath in drugs and alcohol? Does he live a well-balanced system in life mentally, physically, spiritually, and emotionally? If there were a problem in any of those areas

The Epitome of a Player

that I have just mentioned; it would not be a wise choice to engage in a serious relationship or marriage with the man.

Sometimes a man can be well balanced in all four areas, then lose balance in certain areas after getting married. If this happens the two of them should talk to make sure everything is fine. Maybe he was tired from doing overtime on the job and decided to take some time away from the gym. That's ok so long as he picks up the exercise program again at a later date.

This same excessive involvement on his job could slow down the process of taking the woman out a lot (to dinner's, movies, plays, parties, etc). That scenario could affect the mental and emotional balance on the part of both (the woman and the man). That should be talked about and hopefully it will not take long to get back on the right track in those areas. The man will appreciate your concern; and you will feel excellent about yourself and how you handled the entire ordeal.

Now the female non-player is ready to engage in a very fruitful, rewarding, and long lasting relationship with a man. She is ready to improve and enhance the relationship if she is already married. When all is said and done I hope that you will reflect on this chapter and say <u>yeah, the things I read in The Female Non Player chapter were very interesting and very helpful.</u> I will appreciate your acknowledgment and feel very good about it. Thank You.

9

THE MALE NON-PLAYER

Proverbs: 29:22, an angry man stirs up strife and a furious man abounds in transgression.

It is inevitable for the time to come when a street hustler decides he wants to do something different. But what happens to that cold and harsh temper he needed to cultivate in order to survive on the streets? Why take that type of temperament into a relationship with a new woman or wife? So what if you don't consider yourself to be a player anymore.

Many players (especially pimps and macks) beat their women in the past. Just because a man decides not to tag the word player on him anymore doesn't mean the abusive behavior is gone. Street hustlers do not live balanced lifestyles because the use of drugs, alcohol, and cigarettes (presumably) goes along with the territory. For that reason there is no spiritual or physical balance. Many of those hip dudes don't even continue their education.

So, after making a happy meal out of drugs for many years and burning their lives out to the point that a drug treatment program (if they live that long) is their only hope and savior left-they get off drugs and feel they are ready for a relationship with a nice young lady right?

Let's get real! Put that dog gone Godzilla hit down! That's what's making you believe change can happen overnight. There are too many women getting brutally beat and killed by men who have horrendous mood swings (from drug and alcohol use). They can't keep their emotions balanced and many of you men know cotton picking well that you acted as if you entered into a relationship with a gym punching bag instead of a woman.

You have just come out of the outer limits and the twilight zone, so what in this world made you feel that you would change from the almighty hit man overnight? Put that cheap wine down and get rid of that blunt! That's your problem!!! Now get to a drug treatment facility. Even now as you read this book some woman is laid out on the floor after you gave her a roundhouse punch. So now you're ready for a new woman in your life right? Don't forget to buy her a helmet, a bulletproof vest, some boxing gloves, and a mouthpiece (she has to be prepared for you)!

The Epitome of a Player

In order for a man (coming off the streets) to be the epitome of a player, he has to be able to control those negative behaviors that were acquired in the fast lane. Not only should he stay out of a relationship with a woman for at least a year; he should get counseling in order to help with the change in lifestyle. Let the counselor know you were "hit man of the year" with the ladies.

Change is not easy. Many people don't adjust to change very well. It is wise for the ex-player to realize that the nice young lady he is looking for as his companion will have disputes and misunderstandings with him occasionally. That is simply part of love, relationships, and marriage. You are not stepping into the boxing ring when you and your woman have a discrepancy-so don't put the gloves on and come out fighting!

I am going to provide ten questions for the street hustler who has decided to make a change and play it straight. These questions are meant to provide guidance and positive thinking to make the adjustments easy for his new anticipated lifestyle.

1. Have you made up your mind that drugs and alcohol are out of your life for good? It takes a made up mind to avoid the negative decisions that complicated and nearly ruined your lives.

2. Have you made a decision to continue your education in every way possible year after year to rise above your circumstances and stay ahead in life? This question is for those who want more than a just barely making ends meet lifestyle. Remember that couples do fight, argue, kill and steal over money.

3. Have you found a group of people to associate with who have given up drugs, alcohol, and practice the same positive beliefs about a continued education like you? People can ask questions like they did when they found others who used drugs. The same thing applies for finding others who practice abstinence from drug use. Just ask.

4. Have you decided on a relationship with just one sweet woman instead of multiple relationships? Lust is a major problem for way too many of us men. A made up mind is absolutely necessary when making that positive change for the best.

The Male Non Player

5. Do you have a system for managing stress in your life? The use of drugs and alcohol actually causes stress and mixed emotions. It can easily ruin a nice match up between a man and woman.

6. Have you made a decision never to hit another woman if you did so in the past? It is imperative that many men (especially the ex-hustler) look at women in a totally different way if they were physically abusive to them in the past. Women should not be taken advantage of because so many of them are physically weaker than men. It generally takes a real man to learn how to keep his cool under pressure and not take his frustrations out on the woman. It is time to start removing ladies out of shelters for battered women instead of loading them up. Many men should think twice and then walk it off in order to adjust to rational thinking before hitting a woman. She is already at a disadvantage physically. Don't rub it in and be a poor excuse for your mate. The man should think about whom he can call in order to get help. It can be a trusted friend or a drug treatment center if drugs and alcohol is involved. He should remember that he would not want a man hitting his mother, sister, or another female relative of his. So be respectful.

7. Have you found a gym with a whirlpool and steam room, or set up an exercise program at home for relaxation and physical fitness? Many men did whatever it took to come up with the money for drugs on a daily basis. But when they stop getting high they start looking at 35 to 45 dollars a month for a gym membership to be expensive. There are men who spent hundreds of dollars a day on drugs but now look at 35 to 45 dollars a month as expensive. It is difficult for many people to spend money on the appropriate things to do in life like paying bills, buying groceries and taking care of their kids. If you take care of your body, your body will take care of you.

8. Do you have an understanding of spirituality and purpose in life? Proverbs 1:5, a wise man will hear and increase learning, and a man of understanding will attain wise counsel. It will be a good idea for a man to comprehend the book of Proverbs for wisdom

and understanding. After that, it would be advisable for him to seek the counsel of someone much wiser in spiritual knowledge than he, so that a continued approach of a positive direction and intellectual understanding in life can be accomplished.

9. Do you go out to the movies, bowling, roller-skating, ice-skating, dinners, picnics, museums, field trips, basketball games, football games, soccer games, golf matches, tennis matches, Olympic games, or any other forms of amusement/entertainment? A life of drugs and alcohol keep many people confined in one area for one purpose. That purpose is to keep on getting high and then search for more drugs when they run out. It is important to come out of the make believe world of those crazy false hopes and ridiculous fantasies.

10. Have you decided to immediately start working on any of the nine questions that you answered no? A person who answered yes to all nine questions is on his way to a rewarding and fulfilling life. If you need to work on any of those nine questions get started right away, don't delay. It will be worth the time and effort you put into it.

    A down, young player, has to understand, appreciate and give respect in order to receive respect. That's the only way to carry the game the way it has always been presented. Only then can he adjust to those circumstances that call for common sense, dignity, and responsibility.
    The point I'm making right now is that all players are responsible for the babies their women have while they're in his family. That's right! That statement will come as a shock to many young men in the game who were not aware of that. Who do you expect for her to point at as the father of her child if she is out on the streets turning a date with every Tom, Dick and Harry out there? Isn't she turning over all her money to you?
    One of the biggest calamities of the game is when young players new to the game deny a baby by one of his sporting ladies. Is she supposed to be taking names and phone numbers to keep count of every trick she lay up with? Will you young, hip, and too cool to be true players get real?
    The mack game goes back way farther than many of you was born. There are simply too many of you young pimps and macks turning your

The Male Non Player

backs on your women when they have a baby. Then you all will say <u>he is not yours</u>. The baby is yours so stop being so naïve, lame, low lifted, and a dog gone shame to this fast game. It's time for you to stop being so <u>young, confused, cheap</u>, and simply <u>blind</u> to the fact that it's your responsibility to take care of those kids whether she already had them, or got pregnant when you started handling all the money.

Check with a veteran who has been in the game for ten years or more and he will tell you the same thing. There are too many of you young bucks caught up into getting high and being irresponsible in order for you to carry on the dignity and respect of a long time player's game.

And to add insult to injury many of you young hustlers will call yourselves ready for a good woman when you get tired of street life. How can you be ready for a good woman when you didn't live up to your responsibilities while playing the streets? Are you supposed to stop being stingy over night? A good woman doesn't want to change pampers and put a nipple in your mouth boo. She is looking for a mature, responsible man, who can stand up to pressure and do all that he is supposed to be doing as a real man. Take care of your kids while you're in this game. Read this chapter over again before tagging the title of male non-player on yourself. Don't be so quick for a change with a new life and a good wife. You have to be a new man first (at least a year away from women after giving up drugs if you can hold out that long), and that takes time.

I am going to repeat an earlier statement (because redundancy helps people remember) that I made in this book. This time I'm going to put it in a different way because many people don't interpret statements the same way. Some people interpret the same statements better if put in a different way.

The use of alcohol, drugs and cigarettes, started out as something cool, relaxing and entertaining for young people. It was associated with going to football games, basketball games, parties, hanging out on the streets, or at one of their parent's homes. Many young men took things a little farther and realized they had the charisma and conversation that women liked. That made them feel a little above the average young man their age, especially when they would see some young men struggling to get one girlfriend. Pretty soon they learned the ropes and realized that these young ladies would do anything to please them. Eventually these young men started considering themselves to be young players because they each had several women putting money in their pockets. These young

The Epitome of a Player

dudes started feeling on top of the world and nothing else in life mattered. They were macks!

I found it necessary to supply information that is very seldom available to the novice in the street game. Understand that this pimp and mack game has played out. There is simply too much over indulgence in detrimental drugs that has brought on irresponsibility, pre-mature deaths, extensive jail time, confusion, bewilderment, and lost of hope.

I don't care how much you like the pimp and mack style. It doesn't make sense anymore! This is a wake up call to those young people on the streets. There is no such thing as mastering drugs and alcohol. Those narcotics are in the way of your success in the game. The stipulations pertaining to gentlemen of leisure's and men of leisure's (who don't use drugs) have not been available to you. I have given you the information you need about those two styles in this book. Update your game and use that information.

It's also ok if you choose to call yourself a male non-player. That's what this chapter is all about. But you will still need the qualities of the gentleman of leisure and the man of leisure in order to prepare yourself for that good woman you feel that you're ready for. Yeah, that sweetie pie you are so anxious to hook up with will be expecting you to be educated enough to put projects together and make the money fall.

And I'm not talking about illegal projects like the ones you played on the streets. That chapter is not part of your life anymore. Flip the pages. You're on a new chapter now. You will need new and honest ideas for a new and honest woman.

Read over the Gentleman and Man of Leisure chapters. Pay close attention to the areas they practice on continued education. You will also benefit from these two chapters farther in this book: Making Things Happen and The Psychology of a Players Circle.

It's not ok to slow your life down just because you decide to leave the streets and not consider yourself a player anymore. The women that use to be in your different families didn't just choose you for looks only (many of us men don't look so hot anyway).

We get chosen for our intellect also. Our ability to come up with unique ideas and make the money flow non stop-is one of the main qualities we have. Those qualities come from being in the mix with some of the best hustlers in the game. Yeah, leave the drugs and alcohol out, but don't forget your qualities that made life interesting. There are plenty of

The Male Non Player

woman who are hip, quick and smooth, that don't want a deadbeat who has decided to get an average job and sit in front of the television getting fat while watching sports.

If that's the case get a big fat woman who will sit in front of the television with you. She will only be concerned about how much food you bring home. Both of you can get humongous and slimy with fat. Pretty soon neither one of you will be able to fit through the door. And don't worry about sex because both of you will be too big for the man to stick that little thing in you.

The cost of living (especially health care) is way too high for a man to just rely on his looks to get by in a relationship with a woman. And if things don't work out you will run to one of the fellows and say <u>yeah man</u>, she just be thinking about money, money, and more money. She is just no good and greedy.

Wasn't you about money when you was on the streets hustling? The real problem came when you stepped out of a world where money was everything, and then stepped into your own make believe world thinking a woman should accept you as you are, with no money. That's not the real world! That dog gone dope is still frying your brain. Landlords don't take good looks for rent payments. Bills have to be paid and that six-dollar an hour job you went out and got is simply not enough. Get back in school and stop complaining about you don't like to read.

You read every cotton picking Playboy and Hustler magazine on the rack every month but you can't read schoolbooks? Ok, maybe you just looked at the pictures. That's ok; you're not alone. But you know what I'm trying to say. You were about the money on the streets and that don't change when you leave the streets to play it straight. The relationship will work if you will work. Good luck to your new life <u>Mr. Male Non Player</u>!

10

WANNABES, WOULD HAVE BEENS, COULD HAVE BEENS, SHOULD HAVE BEENS, NEVER WILL BE'S, AND MAYBES

There was a time when the word player use to be a dignified terminology. And this saying goes back to the 1960's and 1970's. In most neighborhoods back then if you had jacked your slacks and said <u>I'm pimping</u>, <u>I'm a mack,</u> or <u>I'm a player,</u> you could see the respect in the eyes of those who were watching. They would simply wait to hear you say something clever or foxy (two popular old school terms) out of your mouth after making that bold announcement. Now <u>beware</u>, because the imitators have invaded the Earth. Our lives will never be the same again!

Anybody can jack their slacks and make an announcement as a player of some sort or style. But the way you proved it back then were whether or not you could spit that game (talk very well). There were many players back then who spit it very well. Nowadays, if a man comes in a typical crowd that he hasn't been around too much (or for the first time), and made the same announcement, he would usually get some funny looks, disgusted looks, and then the: I'm tired of hearing that (mess) look.

I basically don't use the word player anymore because that word has been dragged to the ground, stomped on and abused, thrown into the garbage and swept under the rug. That's what this chapter is all about. There are many men who have reached the epitome of a player level- without the drugs and alcohol in their lives. They deserve all the respect that's properly due to them. In order for that to happen, it is necessary for me to weed out, and separate those outrageous imposters who are player impersonators. They have no business representing themselves as real live bonafide players.

Those imposters I'm talking about are the <u>wannabes, would have beens, could have beens, should have beens, never will be's, and maybes</u>. They are everywhere! They live in our neighborhoods. They attend the nearby schools. They hang out on the street corners and they even drive around in cars on the streets. The most shocking part is that many women have had relationships with these aliens from another planet. They have even brought them to their homes to meet their parents. Isn't that a dog gone crazy nightmare? Many parents have had heart attacks-then went into

Wannabees, Would have beens, Could have beens, Should have beens, Never will be's, and Maybes

irreversible shock after meeting these unidentified substances that their daughters call players. I'm surprised the world hasn't self-destructed from a case of outrage and shock!

But it's all right today. You see; I have a solution for the parents of the world and the many women who have discovered that they never had a player. Their lives were almost ruined because of them. I'm going to give a description of the wannabes, would have beens, could have beens, should have beens, never will be's, and maybes. This will make their identification easier with an evacuation plan for getting away from them.

It starts out as a very subtle approach. No one is suspecting this because the young cool breezes are kicking it on a real mellow level and they are simply enjoying another pleasant day. They start out on the corner watching and socializing with the ladies as they walk by. A sexy mama walks by and one of the fellows in our crowd says: <u>hello pretty lady</u> how are you doing today?

The pretty lady just keeps on walking and don't even speak. At that point and time the <u>unthinkable</u> happened. To everybody's amazement the young man who spoke to her picked up a darn bottle and threw it at the sweetie as she kept walking. She stopped and gave him a piece of her mind and he had the nerve to curse the woman out as if she had thrown the bottle at him.

I have just given you a classic example of an unbearable <u>wannabe</u>. He's today's misfortune and tomorrow's disaster. There is one in every crowd of young players. Many readers can think of one in their crowd right now. We were about seventeen years of age when this happened (true story), and we ran the wannabe off the corner. We told him not to come back around. We were totally embarrassed and didn't want ladies thinking that all of us were like that.

The wannabe really, really, really, want to be admired as a player. He fantasize being cool, calm, hip and in the mix like the rest of the <u>young gents</u>. He can easily fool people and start hanging out with them. But he just can't control his insane temper. This dude is a despicable madman who couldn't spell the word finesse-even if somebody spelled the word out loud first. He will still mess it up.

Those wannabes are mesmerized with the attention that the real player's get. They have no problem overplaying their hand by taking a

The Epitome of a Player

bath in cologne and jewelry. Their overly stylish clothes don't match and they will even mess up three wet dreams in one night.

Their need to fit into an elite circle has dominated their personality to the point of shame and insanity. They will do their best to try and get a woman in bed before she finds out about their barbarian behavior. They know it's all over with once the ladies find out that they are undisciplined monsters.

I would like to extend my empathy, understanding, and condolence to the entire parent's who had to suffer with the company of wannabes that your daughters brought home for you to meet. Your daughters just didn't know any better. The wannabes have fooled many people. But now that I have described their argumentative and unbearable personality, it is possible that your daughters will know how to identify them and run for cover when they realize a wannabe is talking to them. And if all else fails she should immediately get to a telephone and call the S.W.A.T. team to take him away. He is a menace to society. Get away from there and go home to pick this book up and then read over the gentleman of leisure chapter again. There is a good player out there for you. Don't give up.

I regret saying that the poor unsuspecting ladies who are looking for a nice young man in their corner are not out of the woods just yet. It is one nightmare to run into the wannabe, but the next shocker would be her running into a-would have been. This is another sad scenario. The-would have-been is a real cool dude who has two or three women putting money in his pockets. He is not argumentative and he is accepted in the player's circle, but the unthinkable happens again! He goes out and commits a burglary and ends up in jail. And when he gets out of the lock up he continues to commit burglaries. His women finally realized that he's disillusioned and told him that he was not a player

Now that's what I call an insult. He didn't even let that bother him. He was committed to living a confused lifestyle of burglary and macking. At some point and time you have to drop one style and choose the other. You can't do both and still be considered a player. The-would have been-never gets that far. I took drastic measures by going to the bathroom and splashing cold water on my face with hope that I would wake up from a nightmare. This couldn't be happening, but it was true. The cold water didn't help. There are many men who can't decide if they want to be a player or a burglar.

Wannabees, Would have beens, Could have beens, Should have beens, Never will be's, and Maybes

I really need to reiterate that there are many women who have fell victim to bringing a would have been home to meet their parents; then had to live with the embarrassment of telling one of her parent's that her man is in jail for burglary. But she doesn't give up because she is convinced that she has a real player as a man.

Then the unthinkable happens again! She ends up standing in front of her parents crying and trying to explain how her man went to jail again for another burglary. At that point and time her parents have a heart attack (like the other parents), and then go into irreversible shock because of what their poor daughter is going through.

It's a real good thing I included this chapter in my book. Now the daughters of many nice parents will know how to identify the-would have been-at some point and time during the relationship. She will have plenty of time to dial 911 on her cell phone and tell the police to just park in her neighborhood for only a few minutes, because there well be a burglary in progress. It is the only thing a woman can do to save the-would have been-from himself, because eventually, he will get shot while climbing through somebody's window. And who knows, he could very easily climb through her parent's window. There is no shame in the-would have beens-game.

There are many men who <u>would have been</u> a player if they had kept accumulating women, receiving money from them, and gave up the burglaries. They could have also copied the gentleman of leisure style at some point and time. But the poor lost souls are misdirected with an off balance personality that's identical to bewilderment.

The players who run into this character in their crowd would do good to tell him to put the burglar tools down and "give it a rest," then direct him to his women and tell him that they are enough for him to make it. If that don't do it; you young men will need to run him off just like we ran the wannabe off; then keep your fingers crossed-hoping that he will never return.

I really wish like heck, I could end this nightmarish, dreadful story, and move on to the next chapter, but the world is still in danger. You would think women have enough on their hands with the wannabes and would have beens, but I suggest that the ladies grab hold of something to keep from passing out on the floor while I tell them that they will eventually run into the-<u>could have been</u>-unless she listen closely to what I have to say.

The Epitome of a Player

He is an exceptionally handsome man. His women will go to bed with him anywhere at any time. He has a nice conversation for the ladies and he has a fair amount of intelligence. If he wanted to he could get plenty of money from women or adjust to the gentleman of leisure style easily. The only problem is that the gentleman of leisure style is not very popular or understood very well. But that was not the-could have beens-main problem. He was too lustful with women to receive money from them. He was more interested in the honey and not the money. He is a fanatical sex fiend.

He is also a purse-snatcher. That's right! I just let the cat out the bag. There were times when he would snatch two or three pocket books at once. He was accepted in the player's circle, but he hung around those hustlers that snatched pocket books. Sometimes he would hang out with the-would have been-and do some burglaries. Yes, there are times when two peas in a pot will get together and do similar crimes. There is a mass confusion going on and the game is losing its dignity.

Sometimes at a later date the-could have been-will try to make a change and organize a flock of women for financial purposes. At that point it's normally too difficult because players learn the tricks of the trade at an early age; not mid-life. Many women have brought the could have been home to meet their parents, but again, they had to let him go in shame because they're parent's had heard of his purse snatching reputation as they fell to the floor and started having seizures with their hands and feet flying wildly in the air. Then they had a heart attack and went into irreversible shock (like the other parent's). One woman didn't want to take a chance of that happening to her parents again. She was also afraid that he might try to snatch her mother's pocketbook one day after she gets better. So she gave him his walking papers and he flooded the room with tears. So she changed his pamper and put a nipple in his mouth.

He could have been a player because he had all the qualities of one. He was simply confused just like the-would have been. If someone runs into a could have been, would you kindly tell him that he can do well as a ladies man if he would give up the purse snatching?

If that word of advice doesn't help-it would be appropriate to put an ad in the newspaper letting the public know what neighborhood the-could have been-is in and what he does. Let the public know he has an irregular personality that will make a sane person throw up, and then, out of shock, jump off the top of an eighty story building. We all have to work

Wannabees, Would have beens, Could have beens, Should have beens, Never will be's, and Maybes

together in order to save the world from these atrocious animals. They have fooled many women into thinking they are players, and have taken away the respect and honor from those who deserve it. Please hang in there with me. We can rescue society together.

I need to repeat the fact that this chapter is about the many out of place characters in society who hit the streets and get totally confused about what they should really be doing out there. They go from one ill-advised venture to the next and they truly believe they are players, but they are not. They are simply hustlers who embarrass the game by being alive. They're existence is a mistake.

It is the public who doesn't know the difference in players and hustlers; then get players confused with burglars, con men, stick up men, purse snatchers, and women beaters. The brutal style of the players who beat women has played out. There are many players who don't hit women and they are not found on the streets. Only the inexperienced hustlers and those who have a hard time changing are found on the streets. They should never, ever, be confused with professional men of leisure's and gentlemen of leisure's.

There was another young man in our circle who had plenty of women liking him and the ladies considered him a cool breeze. Oh yeah, right, tell me another one-then pinch me please! There is a mass confusion among hustlers who are trying to be acknowledged players. They will do something completely out of pocket and contrary to what they are about. All those pretty women would have done anything in the world for him, but he was mesmerized with hold ups

I need a reality check behind that statement. It was never my concern what other hustlers did on the streets when I was out there. It's still not my concern. Right now I'm speaking for the sake of clarity and bringing back respect for the game. I need to continue acknowledging in this book that those who want to be considered a ladies man should stick with women, and those who don't particular care for the players style should not acknowledge himself in that form or fashion, but simply as a hustler.

This gentleman who could have had plenty of money from plenty of women; stuck up bars, dope dealers, and stores. He even liked snatching pocket books with the-would have beens and the-could have beens. He ends up doing a lot of time behind bars. In all actuality, he

The Epitome of a Player

should have been a player, because that's what our neighborhood was made up of. That's where his strong points were.

Some people get infatuated with gangster movies and feel a need to imitate the characters on the movies. The roaring twenties are over with. I don't think it's a good idea to get caught up into living out dangerous fantasies. The jails are already over crowded. There's no room for you! And to add insult to injury you will get out of jail or the penitentiary, and do the same crimes as if you don't have the ability to learn something new.

I am constantly stating that the streets are not an <u>uneducated approach</u> to financial success. It's ok to hang out every now and then to socialize with the homeboys, but always spend some quality time in the schoolbooks. Get some fat in your head. The streets are about game and game is knowledge. It simply has to be understood that knowledge is also in other places besides the streets.

If somebody runs into a-should have been-it would be highly noble of you to tell him to take a break on those stick-ups. He over played it; and if that don't help then you can pass some flyers around to the ladies in the neighborhood stating that the-should have been-has escaped from the insane asylum with saliva running down his mouth and he has outrageous bad breath.

Let them know that he's armed with deadly underarm odor and humongous bumps on his face. Then call the fire department and tell them (when they arrive) to set the-should have been-on fire first, wait a few seconds; then put the fire out.

Hopefully, that will save the ladies from the disaster of unexpectantly having a-should have been-in their life. Please put your lucky rabbit foot on, and then cross your fingers, hoping it will never happen to you.

It seems like a real injustice to continue discussing the shocking personalities of those who have fooled, conned, and slid their way into the unsuspecting lives of many women. I need to do something. I just can't allow these zombies (called impersonators) to continue infesting the earth!

There is something about this next character that brings out the horror surrounding the decisions made by women who choose this type of man. His actions go beyond the call of stupidity. I'm talking about the one and only <u>never will be</u>. I need to catch my breath because this one is a real eye opener.

Wannabees, Would have beens, Could have beens, Should have beens, Never will be's, and Maybes

There are some men who <u>never will be</u> a player even if they tattooed the word player on their foreheads in big capital letters. They are found in crack houses with bowling ball eyes, greasy lips, and turning up a bottle of pimp juice (cheap wine). Many of them have won an award for: <u>geek of the month</u>. They may have escaped from the planet Pluto. The shocker and horror of it all; are the many women who will still choose the-never will be-for a man.

I am truly convinced that a good number of women have had so many wannabes, could have beens, should have beens, and would have beens, in their lives; they decided to throw the towel in and take the next thing that comes their way. The man can be in any shape, form or condition. It just doesn't matter anymore. I consider that to be a real act of desperation, but here goes the low down.

I will start out by talking about the women who took that mountain of a hit from a stolen car antenna, and didn't give a darn about choosing the first creature in sight (with his eyes blood shot and glassy) for a dog gone man. Now how long will that association last? He probably took one of those Godzilla hits and chose you too!

It has got to be obvious that the odds are against the relationship lasting. But oh no! You found love in the crack house right? You didn't find love! You found somebody to help you feed that bent up car antenna you broke off somebody's car. You know good and well both of you can't stand each other when the drugs run out; but when you get another bag its love all over again right?

That's insanity disguised as love in the horror story both of you are living in. Then to top it off, you ladies will have the audacity to tell that never will be; he's a player. He's just a crack head with a few extra dollars until the dope and you run out at the same time.

Stop abusing the game! What makes you think you got a player when he sells everything that's not nailed down (including you) to get money for another hit? And you ladies will take that jack in the box alien from another planet-home to meet your parents. You just blew it right then and there!

You will never, ever, be able to convince your parent's again that you have met a very nice young man who has it all together. Especially with him sitting there looking like the wolf man with nappy hair sticking straight up, blood shot eyes, and spilled wine on his clothes. Who's going

The Epitome of a Player

to pay the doctor bills because of your parent's having heart attacks, seizures, and then irreversible shock after meeting the extraterrestrial you brought home? Can you really afford it?

For now on when that kind of ill advised relationship fail in your life, don't go picking up the telephone to call your girlfriends and say players ain't about nothing! Yon knew the man was not a player! You were only mad because he ran out of ideas for coming up with more quick money to keep feeding your burned black antenna. So you got rid of him.

Now I would like to discuss the situation about women who either don't like to get high or they don't get high on crack. I don't want any of you ladies to feel left out. As a matter of fact, after you too, have had a relationship with every scum bag, sleaze, zip fool; scum of the earth and whatever the ground would cough up, you too will choose the <u>never will be</u> out of panic that it may take awhile to find a good man and you needed to get your groove on.

Don't say it isn't so; because you know darn well you'll be telling a lie to the point of not being able to look at yourself in the mirror. And your mirror will blow up if your <u>never will be</u> a player, look into it. Oh, so many endless stories about how women pick all the men who are bad and no good for them. The ladies excuse for that mis-judgment is that he's intriguing or he's funny.

Well all that's fine and dandy. Just admit that truthfully when you are socializing with your girlfriends and you all start putting player's down. In actuality, you've been choosing every bad apple, misfit, and degenerative unknown species from other planets that accidentally landed on earth.

Those never will be's you ladies pick out (with no shame about yourselves) are something out of the ordinary that not only can't spell the word player, but will stutter trying to pronounce it. This is the time for many women to start acknowledging that there have always been qualified gentlemen players in the game, but the majority of them are normally taken or married by the time you get to them. "<u>THE TRUTH WILL SET YOU FREE</u>."

The never will be's (from other planets) are creatures that don't go to the gym or engage in any form of exercise at all. They don't like reading unless it's one of those naked girly books (and they only look at the pictures). They may pick up the newspaper every now and then in order to read the comic section (then they are through).

Wannabees, Would have beens, Could have beens, Should have beens, Never will be's, and Maybes

They frequently do drugs and alcohol with an occasional cigarette in their mouth to look cool, calm, and collected. But in actuality, they are an emotional mess with no sound spiritual concepts and poor health, because they replace food with drugs. The best quality that the never will be's have-is the great ability to woo the ladies. He is the epitome of lust.

Many times have I heard real players look at the man a woman is with and say: how in the heck did he get her? The never will be's are quick to take a shower and a bath in sex. They are not a challenge for the women to get in bed; which lets the ladies know he is a sure thing. He could very easily be: "the yes man" of the ladies. Such is the case with the never will be's. The women know that the relationship will not last, but he's the nip in the bud until she gets the man she really wants.

In many cases women are tired of chasing after a man that many other women want, because numerous men of this caliber can't make up their minds on one woman. So she does what she can with someone else (a never will be) until the person she really wants is ready to commit or until she can find someone other than him with the same (or very close to it) qualifications.

The never will be; is someone extremely difficult to get off drugs, get back into school, and explain spiritual concepts to; because he has made up in his mind to enjoy the party scenes made up of women, drugs, booze and pills. Even if he does think about a change, it is too difficult for him to do it, because the alien never was strong in stamina, emotions, and effective decision-making.

Sometimes he can make a few adjustments like playing basketball, jogging, doing push ups, and making inquiries about getting back in school. But he soon slips back into his old mode, and forty years later you will see him standing on the same corner with a wine bottle in his hand, trying to bum a cigarette. It is simply not meant for everyone to make it off those streets no matter how hard they try. Only those who never give up on making a positive change will succeed, but they got less time than they think.

If someone happens to run into a person of this character and recognize the signs of <u>never will be</u> written all over his face, walk, talk, and attire; do yourself a favor and just keep on walking; even if you know him personally. It's ok to speak to him (if nobody is looking), and then move on before he starts talking because part of his characteristics could rub off on you. And you definitely don't want that to happen. Another reason for moving on is because some nice young ladies may see you socializing with him and then put you in a category, which means you will have a difficult time trying to explain to the ladies how you got to know him.

The typical never will be; won't ask for help until after he has lost everything; have no place else to stay, and have simply passed out on the street. At that point and time, the paramedics came and rose above the impossible dream. They just saved society with a miracle solution that healed him (a hard slap in the face). Now he is approachable because he will have a new walk, talk, and a new set of clothes. You may run into one who miraculously recover and make it. And by golly, you may even be proud to be seen with this one.

This last person is someone I am kind of proud to talk about. He has risen above drugs. He is in school, has a girlfriend or a wife and kids, and is well on his way to success in the world. He goes to the gym and exercise, (maybe lifts weights) jogs and gets in the whirlpool and steam room. This, along with a thorough understanding and practice of spiritual concepts, leave him relaxed with inner peace and fortitude. He has joined a book club and has started reading a collection of self-help books. He even meditates whenever possible for emotional control. What a gigantic change from the lifestyle of street hustle, drugs, and indecision in life.

There is only one apparent draw back to this character that I call the maybe. The change in his lifestyle isn't so easy and many hustlers who have made it this far for ten or more years have slipped up and fell back into that old lifestyle that kept them down. But all eyes are on him because he is doing the unthinkable. He rose above the odds after his family and friends gave up on him. People who haven't got that far are watching him. Those players who have made it got their eyes on him as a potential up and coming bonafide gentleman player who is worthy of an induction into their circle.

Unlike the should have been who was doing good for ten years and slid back into the streets picking up his destructive habits again, the maybe has lasted longer than that and is still going strong. He simply has to remember that there is no looking back and no slip-ups to be made. He has exhibited much more stamina in his daily balance (mentally, physically, spiritually, and emotionally) than the-should have been who was basically weak in his balance and never got a chance to fortify it. If you ever run

Wannabees, Would have beens, Could have beens, Should have beens, Never will be's, and Maybes

into a maybe, just compliment him on his positive lifestyle change and wish him the best of luck in his conquest for popularity, fame, and success. A little support and encouragement is all he need every now and then. You never know what may happen from there. I mean <u>maybe</u>, just <u>maybe</u>, he will be a true player one day.

I would hope that this chapter would be one step into a process of women looking at the word player in a different light. It's not fair to those qualified hustlers who have worked hard over the years to not only keep a balanced lifestyle, but to also be a better man for a good woman.

It is important to remember that every man is not who he says he is just because he jacks his slacks and announce himself as a gentleman of leisure or any of the other styles I mentioned. People can size hustlers up a lot better because of the information I just provided in this chapter. The imposters and impersonators of the game don't have to fool you anymore.

I hope that I have left you with the thought of having more respect for real players. Hopefully, the game has become a lot more respectable with the breakdown of the gentleman of leisure and man of leisure. My everlasting thanks and best wishes go out to you again.

11

PLAYERS AND THE PENITENTIARY

Well, I'm at another turning point in this book, where as, I have to look reality in the face. I have talked about the dangers of being on those streets without a balanced lifestyle. There are too many pitfalls of drugs, alcohol and crime. So in spite of those traps, many people will always choose to take their chances in a fast, controversial hustle, of wit and con on the streets.

Even with the advice I gave about having money put away in order to bail you out of jail, hustlers will still shrug their shoulders with little or no pocket money; and take their chances anyway. Those hustle and con games on the streets are like the kleptomaniac who has an obsessive desire to steal. There is just something about the challenge of taking chances that could send you to the graveyard or the penitentiary. It's the thought of rising above all the obstacles and traps of the fast lane that seem to make the risk worth taking.

Normally when people are going back and forth to the county jail, department of corrections, and the neighborhood jail cells; it is a sure sign that they are very close to catching a case and ending up doing time in the penitentiary which is called the big house. It is my intent in this chapter to prepare many unsuspecting young people for survival in the big house- should they end up there at some point and time. This is part of the necessary adjustments to be all that you can be as a player in this game.

The penitentiary is a place that separates the men from the boys and the women from the girls. It is a place where one has to look death in the face and show no fear. Many hustlers on the street beat their fists on their chest, then flash their guns and knives while verbally expressing how down and tough they are about their game (which is whatever hustle they engage in).

The first thing they learn (if they haven't been to the big house before) is that nobody in there is tough, because nobody knows what the next person know, or what the next person will do. So it's best for people to go in there and watch what they say out of their mouth (because saying the wrong thing can get you killed).

Players and the Penitentiary

They will need to look in the mirror when they get to their cells and practice on making a crazy face. It is appropriately to have a look so detrimental that other inmates will think you're ready to kill one of them if they make the slightest wrong move.

I was in a cell one time with one of my many cellmates in Pontiac Penitentiary (many of the cell mates will go home or transfer to other areas depending on what job they decided to take, or they may transfer to another penitentiary), because cellmates come and go. This particular cellmate (sometimes called celli) had classified himself as a killer on the streets. He told me that I did not have a killer's instinct. He told me that he couldn't see the look to kill in my eyes and if I intended on making it out of Pontiac alive I needed to come up with a look to kill. He said I needed to be prepared to kill somebody if necessary.

Then he said when people fight in the big house they are not trying to hurt the other person; they are trying to kill the other person (no witness no case). So when I was alone in the cell I would look in the mirror and practice different crazy looks until I came up with one that I considered to be a suitable look to kill; and it worked. Every now and then somebody would say to me. Man, you look like you're ready to kill somebody. And I would say: I feel like killing somebody right about now; and I would keep a pen, pencil, or any type of sharp object in my pocket in case I seriously got into a fight and had to stab somebody. Practically anything could be used as a weapon. Some inmates carried knives that they got from the cafeteria while eating. Some con's made their own knives (called shanks) when they were on their jobs at a workshop on the grounds.

It is very common for inmates to look over their shoulders every now and then to make sure that some crazy maniac is not coming from behind in order to stab them (usually in the head, stomach or back). A person in the big house don't have to do anything wrong in order to get killed. Some out of control serial killer or madman may stab you because he simply doesn't like your looks or personality (unless you established some kind of look to kill about yourself). It could very easily happen in the summer time when inmates are hot and irritable.

Every kind of hustler, con man, gangster, rapist, killer, pervert, cutthroat and sleaze is in the penitentiary. You simply don't know whom to trust. The best policy is not to trust anyone because there is always someone waiting for another inmate to show a sign of fear or weakness, in order to take advantage of that person. There is something about the

The Epitome of a Player

frustrations of being locked up in tiny jail cells away from society for a long period of time that cause people to build up ill feelings and anxiety. They have a tendency to do little nit picky things to bug people. That's one of the ways they relieve themselves of frustrations from being locked up.

The agonizing part about someone getting on your nerves is that you will be tempted at times to beat the mess out of a person or stab him. But you don't want to take a chance on losing your good behavior time which means you can get your sentence shortened if you stay out of trouble (or lengthened depending on the offense). So there will be many days when you will have to bite the bullet, hold your breath, count to ten and then exhale nice and slow for relaxation. You really don't need any additional time behind bars.

At this point and time, I find it necessary to elaborate on males going to the big house since I obviously have never been sentenced to a female penitentiary (if so, I would have asked for a life sentence), and can't extend any meaningful information about that situation. I'm quite sure the experiences are similar.

There is something of a serious game played on young men coming into the big house for the first time. When I was walking in the long double line of con's coming through those big steel doors of Pontiac when we first arrived off the sheriff bus, we had to walk by the yard where there were inmates lifting weights, jogging, walking and talking. There were a few inmates standing by the fence in the yard watching us walk by; and they were pointing at the young guys in the line and saying out loud: <u>that's going to be my kid!</u> They were talking about whom they would turn out (mainly white guys with long hair), and use for sexual intercourse.

I use to think that the white guys with long hair was the only males who hurried up and cut their hair short before coming to their cells. It didn't take very long for me to realize that even African American males with long hair coming down to their neck or shoulders would get their hair cut short. It is a myth to think that white males were the only one's who had to worry about that.

There are truly, some inmates, who have been locked up so long; a handle with a mop head on it will look like a woman to them. The longer the con's incarceration has been-the more his mind has changed. It doesn't make a darn difference if a person is black, white, Mexican, Puerto Rican, Arab; or a race that no one could figure out. If a sick-minded con looks for a way to molest a person, he is typically going to take advantage of the convict who shows fear in his eyes.

Many young men would ask to be placed in protective custody that is a separate cell house for whoever was too frightened to go into the regular population of inmates. The ones that usually go into protective custody don't come out as often as the other inmates. They will go to the cafeteria, the yard, and to the movies at different times in order to stay away from the regular crowd. They are considered to be wimps, punks, and less than a man, but they don't care because they fear for their lives.

There are some brave young guys who decide to take a chance (even though they're scared to death) because they don't want to be labeled as a wimp or a punk. So what happens every now and then is that one of them will talk about how he was pimping when he was on the streets.

It doesn't make a difference who you may be in there; everybody has to talk about what they were doing on the streets once you get inside of the big house. Even if you don't want to talk about it-the inmates are going to keep asking questions until you talk about your make up. They want to make sure you're not a crank or zip fool who may snap one day and stab somebody in the back. You could also be a "snitch" trying to get information for "five o." You will have to open your mouth and talk.

When bully inmates find out that a young person is calling himself a pimp; they typically invite him into one of the cells to get high off some marijuana. Then they give him snacks for the munchies. After the young pimp gets comfortable and the conversations start moving along pretty smooth between everyone, a big bully in the crowd says to the young pimp, "So you were pimping on the streets huh?" Then the young pimp says, "Yes" (with a naive grin on his face from being high). Then the big bully says: "**Do you know that a pimp will turn a date with another man if necessary to survive if he loses all his women and don't have any other hustle going on for him?**"

Right then and there the young pimp gets silent not knowing what to say because he realizes that he just got tricked and don't know how to get out of the jam. Then the bully says to him: "**You are in this cell with no women or hustle; so now you will have to turn a date in order to survive!**" Sometimes the young guy will say: "No" and then get the mess slapped out of him. Then the young pimp is shaking as he pulls his pants and shorts down. He then bends over so the bully can sexually assault him.

The Epitome of a Player

After that the young guy becomes the bully's kid (and whore for inmates that want him). The bully assaults him sexually whenever he gets ready; and then passes him around to different cells so his inmate friends can molest him. In return, they will give the kid's man (the bully) money, snacks, cigarettes; marijuana, alcohol, pills, drugs, clothes or whatever the bully will accept for the services his kid provide. The kid also does other chores for the inmates. He will wash their underwear and socks, mop their floors, wipe their walls down and even give them oral sex. In other words, they turned him into a real male whore.

Sometimes the young guy starts liking the sex as a way of mentally coping with it. At other times the victim is so humiliated and depressed-to the point where as he eventually hangs himself in a cell when he is alone. But it's not long before the bully finds himself another kid; and he has no remorse over the kid who hung himself.

I have some advice for those young people who will not take my suggestions (about a legal and honest approach to being a man of leisure or gentleman of leisure), and end up in the big house. It will be wise to represent yourselves as a mack, and not as a pimp. It's also a good idea to go over the chapter called: The Mack. Reading over that chapter will give you a thorough understanding of that style and makes it easy to explain the macks style if it becomes necessary while doing a lot of time.

To be the epitome of a player in life is to triumph over all negative circumstances in the game and make a happy ending out of it. That's when the big home, nice car, fantastic wife, nice clothes, vacations, your own business and control of your leisure time take place.

I represented myself as a mack in the big house. I broke the game down well enough so no one would be able to question my knowledge and experience in the game. But I still got into a fight every now and then. It is practically impossible to go through life in a penitentiary without someone challenging you, or without losing your temper and whacking somebody a few times.

The fights didn't bother me because I fought a lot on the streets. For some reason I got into a lot of fights starting in grammar school. Then I would practice boxing with my friends. By the time I was sixteen I was a pretty good fighter. I'm advising young people to practice boxing with their friends because you will never know when you may have to fight someone.

Players and the Penitentiary

It would also be advisable to have money saved up to put on the books so you will be able to spend more than the ten dollars a month that the state gives to you. It would be even better to save enough money to bond yourself out and pay an attorney to beat your case. This player's game is a business and not the "happy go lucky" fan club.

I am reminding young people again that they are considered to be a grown adult when they hit the streets. Don't expect a relative or anyone else to foot the bill if you take a bust. Too many young people are getting disappointed with that kind of irresponsible approach to the streets. Put money to the side to get yourself out (you can't depend on others). If you don't have any money you should stay in jail and simply deal with it.

The man of leisure and gentleman of leisure lifestyles in the game may be a little too complicated for a novice to explain to someone in the penitentiary. He also may not have been living the luxurious lifestyle of those gentleman styles while he was on the streets. It is very beneficial not to lie, because you can very easily run into someone who knew you on the streets. They will tell the other inmates if you're lying. Then you're in big trouble.

It is beneficial to go to the yard twice a day, six days a week, and pump iron. I did that faithfully and size gets respect in the penitentiary. Trust me; a con would rather go up against someone half your size if you got big muscles from pumping iron (even though some don't care about your size).

Some people will join religious groups or gangs in order to have support if they run into problems. Even though religious groups and gangs help their members, it is still wise to be realistic about the fact that you are in the joint with convicts who committed crimes. Many of those crimes were heinous. So still be on guard because someone in your group may try you out if they believe there is a chance for them to molest someone. Some inmates are really sick after being locked up for awhile. So for that reason (believe it or not), some men really do look like women to inmates who have been locked up a long time. Remember that many cons haven't seen a real woman from the outside of the joint for a good minute. A person's mind will seriously change after being locked up for awhile.

I also need to mention that some gangs are very leery of people joining up with them if they were not already gang members on the streets. The gang members simply think that you are taking unfair advantage of them just to be able to have protection and survive in the big house. They

The Epitome of a Player

don't believe you will continue to be a gang member when you get out (even though some people do remain gang members when they get out, many of them don't). They may or may not accept you.

Some gangs take in people who were not gang members on the streets and some don't. If they do accept you it should be acknowledged that you may or may not receive respect from them because they will know that you are faking in the game. Eventually, many of the members will get use to you and kick it with you on the real side.

Always be honest. Don't try and pretend you were in a gang on the streets before you came in the joint, because the gang members will ask you a lot of questions about gang prayers, gang signs, and what specific areas did you hang out in. They will suggest that you should know certain people if you hung out in certain neighborhoods. Besides that, they just might run into somebody who knew you on the streets and that person will admit that you were never in a gang. Then you will have big problems to deal with. You could get roughed up pretty bad for lying so stick to the truth.

There is always a group of players in every penitentiary who hang out together because players are everywhere. If you were a player on the streets with women who were down for you; then you can hang out with those who did the same thing you did.

The best policy in any case is to pump iron six days a week and socialize with those who hustled the way you did on the streets. You don't want to be faking it in that area either, because the players will ask you questions about the neighborhoods you played. They will want to know about people you knew and how you laid down your game (where you put your women to work). They will listen very closely to every word you say to see if you can spit game (talk very cool, clever and experienced).

It is important for those young people on the streets who never been to the penitentiary to think about what they will say to the other inmates in case it ever happens (and hopefully it will never happen). My homeboys and I would discuss the ins and outs of survival while in the penitentiary (the same way I discussed it in this chapter). We were teenagers during that time, and I didn't expect to take a bust and go to the penitentiary, but I listened anyway. The information paid off because I knew exactly how to play it when I got to Pontiac. Never take any information for granted that you learn on the streets and in life as a whole.

Players and the Penitentiary

As time moves on you will find yourselves in various situations when everything you learned (while you were a teenager) becomes valuable.

I will repeat again that this book: <u>The Epitome of a Player</u>, is about saving lives by rising above your negative circumstances in order to be the successful player, hustler, or the non-player you were meant to be. It is imperative that young people who end up in the slammer continue their education by reading as many self-help books as possible.

There are many good books that are motivational and informative material. Good subjects to study in that area would be: effective decision making, building up vocabulary, speech, empowerment and facilitation. Also try: assertiveness, typing, English, Spanish, job interviewing skills, mastermind groups, transcendental meditation techniques, computer skills; communication skills, and anything that picks up your interest that can help you in the job market.

Independent contracting and entrepreneurial-ship work is definitely a player's delight. Just be prepared to work hard. Even if you get life in prison you can still go to law school while incarcerated and learn how to contact attorneys on the outside that can help with your appeal.

Life is always a never-ending hustle and bustle. This player's game is definitely not for the weak, weary, dumb; and the easily discouraged person. I know you're not in that category. I never heard of anyone saying that street hustlers are not intended to be an intellectual group of people. I find it very complimentary in regards to inmates who get their G.E.D, bachelors and masters while locked up or when they get out. They should start working on it before they end up getting a lot of time.

Those degrees will open up doors for them to elevate their game to a higher level. That's what street life is all about anyway. Young people who are hustling on the streets while reading this book should think about where they are at educational wise. Start preparing to elevate your game to a higher level.

Don't go out the door backwards by getting a bachelors or masters, and then decide you want to open a legitimate business and use it as a front to sell drugs. Would you please give me a darn piece of mind! Was drug dealing one of your college classes? Why get an education that good just to help destroy the lives of many young people by putting that poison in their hands? Don't you realize that bankers will be practically breaking their necks trying to give you multi-million dollar business loans because

The Epitome of a Player

you earned your degree? Just make sure you put that business proposal together very well. Your education qualifies you to do that.

A person with a bachelors or masters can make much more money legally than illegally! There are many millionaires and billionaires who have large investments in real estate, stocks, bonds, commodities and entrepreneurial investments. They will not have to worry about the police breathing down their neck because of illegal activities like selling drugs; so why be the old schools fool?

High school dropouts are quick to sell drugs. Why get a college degree and do the same thing that high school dropouts do? You are only proving that you're a <u>sophisticated lunatic</u> wasting a degree! That's going out the door backwards like the wannabe.

Remember what I said about the-would have been-who had lived a well-balanced life, but was an ineffective decision maker. He came up in a typical street lifestyle around a mixture of hustlers and he chose to be a burglar instead of a player. You don't need to do anything illegal to play the game. It can be played legally or illegally. Use your wisdom and be legal. Just understand that the game is not only on the streets, but off the streets too. Elevate your style, pull away from the streets and excel in legal business ventures. You will make more money that way.

The point I'm making is that when you get a bachelors or masters you break away from that old crowd and find those who are as educated as you are (or close to it). Hang out with them. That saying is no disrespect to your old homeboys; it's simply all about progress. Nothing stays the same in life; things change. When things change, you will need to change also. It's as simple as that.

The best person to decide what your life is going to be like is you. Don't ever let anyone make those choices for you. The final decision is always yours. Nothing's wrong with stopping to speak and then socialize with the old crowd for a few minutes every now and then. You don't want to be rude; but you need to move on in order to network with your new associates who are presently putting together multi-million dollar business proposals.

Don't sweat yourself and don't sweat the game. It's all about working smarter and not harder. You don't have to go to the penitentiary, sell drugs, or do anything illegal in order to be down in the game. Think about your wife and kids (the average man has kids) or your girlfriend and kids. What are they suppose to do if you end up doing a lot of time behind bars? Think about that before it actually happen. Don't wait until it happens and then slap your forehead with the palm of your hand and say: what a fool I was! Be a sweet Mack that's cool, calm, collected, and too good to be true. Be a good father and a positive role model for all kids. Give children good advice and good direction in life. Good things will definitely come your way for doing it. Our kids are a blessing and you can only gain blessings for yourself by steering them in the right direction. It will be the best decision you made in your entire life.

    It will be a good point to get readjustment counseling after being in the penitentiary for a year or more. Haven't you noticed that about 75% of people who get out of the penitentiary end up right back in there in about a year (or less)? You are not the same person who stepped into that cell a year ago (or however long you were there).

    You have been exposed to every kind of killer, madman, zip fool, lunatic, manic depressant, crack heads, and just down right crazy son of a guns from all over the world. You have heard many of their crime stories and now you are a better failure than you were before you went in. The itch to try out those unscrupulous schemes will hit you after you hit the streets with your freedom again. You will need to use logic and realize that if those ideas were so hot, the people you got them from wouldn't be locked up. Either way it goes, you had to adjust your thinking from that of a civilian who had his freedom, to that of an incarcerated con who had to seriously plant the thought in his mind about killing someone or beating the heck out of the person until he was at least close to dead.

    The object in the big house is to kill the person you fight, because dead bodies can't be a witness against you in court. That means you won't have to worry about the victim stabbing you in the back with a knife for revenge when you least expect it.

    The prison officials who release you when your sentence is served will not tell you to seek counseling to readjust back into society. It is not their job to tell you that. Readjustment counseling should probably be mandatory but who will foot the bill if the state doesn't? A trusted friend can help in that area or come up with a source for you to go to. Don't be afraid to ask for help. Nobody in this world made it on his or her own without getting help in some form or fashion every now and then. Believe it or not, another aspect of being the <u>epitome of a player</u> (you were meant to be) is to learn how to be humble and down to earth. It is time for a new way of thinking and a new way of living.

12

PLAYERS AND POWER

As I write this book I continuously see the faces of hustlers and young players who are very intelligent, but lack the capacity to get the things done in their life that's most important to them. Therefore, I am going to give them direction in the choices of their desires so they can be the man they want to be in their lives and in their loved ones eyes. Power has to be understood before it can be utilized. <u>Knowledge</u> is the biggest form of power that a person can possess. The more knowledge you have the more power you have. But if you don't use the knowledge effectively then you have no power.

Players are some of the biggest abusers of power because many of them don't understand what power is, how to attain it, and how to use it appropriately when they do acquire it. Remember what I said in the last chapter about someone acquiring a degree and then making a decision to open up a business and make a front out of the business to sell drugs?

That is a good example of abusing power. And don't forget about the young people who drop out of high school to hit the streets and hustle. They want that game up under their belt. It's their desire to learn as much as they can on those streets. I stated earlier in this book that knowledge is acquired from everywhere. It's obtained in schools, libraries, workshops, books, tapes, newspapers, magazines, and from other people. So why are young people dropping out of schools where the knowledge is at? Isn't knowledge game and game is knowledge? They simply don't understand the power they will acquire by sticking with school and learning all they can. I hope this chapter will help.

I am going to discuss three definitions of power that I got from Webster's II New Riverside University Dictionary: 1. <u>The ability or capacity to act or perform effectively</u>. 2. <u>Strength or force exerted or capable of being exerted; might</u>. 3. <u>The ability or official capacity to exercise control over others</u>.

The first definition is the ability or capacity to act or perform effectively. In order to accomplish this; a person should be an effective decision maker. That mean he will have to understand where power comes from and how to use it when it manifest itself.

Players and Power

Power is your knowledge that's stored in the subconscious mind, which is the unlimited storage place for the acquisition of unlimited knowledge (knowledge and power are relentless). The more knowledge that is stored away, the more power a person has. When a decision has to be made the subconscious sends the information to the conscious mind in order to produce the results; in many cases the subconscious mind will send several choices for the conscious mind to choose from. For example: a person is deciding whether to stay in school or drop out to hustle on the streets and make money. The subconscious mind sends these choices: 1. <u>Finish high school and go to college.</u> 2. <u>Go to a trade school after high school.</u> 3. <u>Go to work after high school and save money for</u> college. 4. <u>Deal drugs and make some quick money; buy a nice car, home, nice clothes, and party a lot.</u> So you decide to pick choice number four, which is to deal drugs. You have not made an effective decision because you didn't think about the least risks involved in each choice in order to produce the best results. The biggest risk would be to deal drugs because you increase your chances of losing your life or ending up in jail. Why go broke paying attorneys lots of money to beat your cases?

You will have to watch out for the stick up man and you can't put the money in the bank. You can easily lose your house, car, and other material possessions; then you will develop a drug habit and end up in rehabilitation. In other words, you simply made a decision to make your life difficult. You won't be a role model for your kids and you will not be able to spend much time (if any) with them. It is a foolish decision that carries no constructive power and it is a waste of your life.

An experienced and wise player understands power and exercises it with decisions that will enable him to more easily control his own destiny. He understands that the more knowledge he takes in, the better equipped he will be to run his own business. He will spend more time with his kids; travel and save lots of money; and have a rewarding future with a lovely wife. The first three choices will enable him to do that; and it will put him in the position to meet other people who share the same beliefs that he does.

There's power with change. When players communicate with the same people in the same neighborhoods-they are coming up with the same information year after year. If the information they are coming up with is not producing positive results in their lives then it is time to make a change. Try moving into a new neighborhood and meet new people. You

The Epitome of a Player

should be doing new activities and producing new ideas that were not available to you in the old neighborhood around the old associates.

The subconscious mind will only feed your conscious mind the exact information that you will need for solving problems in your current circumstances. It doesn't have a need to send any new information to you if you're not doing anything new. The first of the three choices will put you in a position of acquiring additional knowledge and meet new people with new ideas.

It has got to be clearly understood that a player relies heavily on a continuous flow of fresh ideas so that he can keep implementing new projects for the acquisition of financial gain. A professional in the game will not stay in one area too long, even if he has a home in that area. More than likely he will have residences in other cities along with his own vacation resorts. The subconscious mind will be forced to dig up new information that it had stored away; and then send it to the conscious for analyzing, and then an application for progress and financial results.

There is power in the word belief. This is another area of effective decision making when a person chooses to believe that he can accomplish anything he want to in this life. But I will not tell you that all you need to do is believe in yourself and then positive things will happen. Something different has to happen in your life in order for belief to be a power tool to be used by you.

The power of change will go hand in hand with the power of belief. In other words, if you believe that you can rise above the pitfalls of the streets, crime and drugs, but don't make a change from hanging out with those who do crimes and drugs, then you might as well take belief and throw it out the window. If you believe that you can make a lot of money through real estate investments or sales, but don't go to school for real estate sales or buy books and tapes that will teach you about real estate investing, well then, you might as well try something different because it will not work.

Action is another power tool that goes hand in hand with your change. It is really not enough to acknowledge that you need to make a change, but don't actually do it. If you believe (the power of belief) that you have the skills for a singer, dancer, actor, broker, teacher, artist, or entrepreneur; then get up right now and pick up a telephone, and make an appointment to talk to somebody about helping you get started.

Players and Power

If you believe that you can rise above drugs, alcohol, and your cigarette addition; then stop what you're doing and pick up the telephone right now, and call a drug rehabilitation center. You can start getting rid of bad habits by replacing them with new and positive goals. Then you can meet new and positive people. Take action right now to make that change. Don't wait! It's been on your mind for quite some time so make that move right now.

This second definition of power that I'm going to discuss is: 2. Strength or force exerted or capable of being exerted. There's vast power in exercise. It doesn't make a difference what kind of business a person opens up; he will not be able to hang in there without good health. This is especially true when a person starts getting older. The heart and bones get weaker unless a person does cardio and strength training. Exercise is also good for keeping the mind strong, sharp, and alert. Power from reading is a good exercise that strengthens the mind and keeps it sharp and focused.

Meditation is a good exercise for relaxation and controlling your emotions. It would certainly be extremely difficult to be successful in any business if a person does not know how to control his or her emotions. The unwise use of harmful drugs and alcohol, hinder your growth, and will damage balanced emotions, effective decision-making, and positive communication with other people. Narcotics have ruined many businesses and have also been the breakdown of many families. Weightlifting is an excellent exercise for strengthening the bones and building up endurance.

There is admiration about the strength that is evident in a person's personality when he speaks, walks, and conducts his business. A spiritual balance helps tremendously in that area. There is positivism and stamina in ones demeanor when he can express himself in all areas of life. He knows whom he is and exactly what he wants to do in life. He has sure steps. He is not walking around as if he is lost in space. He doesn't complain about being tired as if he is struggling to go on in life. As a matter of fact, he can always squeeze more work in his life if need be. There is an old saying that: if you want to get something done-just asks a busy person. I believe in that old saying and I also believe that the busy person you ask is also a strong person, otherwise how could he stay so busy?

It is up to the player to honor the game and be the strong person that he was meant to be. Stop destroying your body and mind with drugs and alcohol. This is especially true for the street hustler because narcotics

The Epitome of a Player

go along with that territory. It is important to remember that when you are out there in the fast lane jacking your slacks and your mack, you are representing a game that has always been meant for the wise and the strong.

It was never a program that was meant for the weak, weary, and strung out drug user. Don't embarrass yourself and those who are carrying the game high by not living a balanced lifestyle and producing positive results. People should be able to see the strength and hope in your profile. Live up to your expectations by being the man you were meant to be.

The third and last definition of power I will discuss is: 3. The ability or the official capacity to exercise control over others. This control factor is a very dangerous area in a player's game because he is actually in control of the lives of many women. So I am basically talking about the pimp and mack who are the only two that organize a family of women for financial and material gain.

The outcome of the future lives of the women, as well as a final destination for the player himself; is typically not discussed on the streets. The game is basically introduced to young people as a way of having several women, drugs, alcohol, a life of going to parties; and living in that world on a daily basis. There is no talk or any acknowledgement that the lifestyle they are living is simply a phase that they are going through. There is a better system for making a living and having a good time that was not available to them.

Many young men are receiving money from women, and then buy plenty of drugs to use while having plenty of sex. They don't have the slightest idea of what to do when eventually; everybody will start getting strung out on those drugs, arguing with each other, getting kicked out of apartments, and they soon split up. At this point they are headed to: "<u>who knows where</u>."

It is important for the player to realize that he entered a hustler's business (legal or not), and everybody should benefit. What difference does it make if you got three women putting money in your pockets and all four of you are walking around everyday with blood shot eyes from drug use? Why stumble around all bent over as if you're about to fall flat on your face any day now? I don't think that would be called running a business. I believe we can look at you all as addicts living it up in drugs and sex until there is no more money.

Players and Power

At some point and time there won't be any hopes left in your life accept finding a quick way to a drug rehabilitation center. And that's the message in this last definition of power. It is a wise suggestion that you players who have women out there playing the streets (with all your lives dominated by drugs); sit down and have a heart to heart talk with your ladies.

Be serious about the played out style of the pimp and mack. Explain to your ladies that nothing stays the same and change will always be there. All of you should read over my chapters again about the man of leisure, gentleman of leisure, and lady of leisure lifestyles-that consist of successful business people living a drug free life.

The pimp or mack, that is the leader, and has control over the entire family; will have to formulate a wise initiative. He must make mature and responsible decisions by discussing the future whereabouts of his women. Everyone that's in the family has to make sensible resolutions on the appropriate change and sensible direction for their lives. This change will not happen overnight. Change takes time, so be patient. Drug rehabilitation and wise guidance from rehab counselors will be necessary. The players should not be nonchalant about losing any of their women to drugs. His position is a very responsible and mature one, which calls for effective decision-making and his strong leadership skills. The change away from the fast lane is inevitable. It has to happen and should take place during the reading of this book if the process hasn't already started. The player should also realize that all of his women will not be open-minded to a change in lifestyle. It won't matter what kind of book they read or who will make that suggestion to them. Drugs are powerful and extremely difficult to give up.

The pimp or mack should simply do their job by breaking up the family and directing everybody in a positive direction for the attainment of higher education and legal business ventures. The players do not want a reputation for not being capable of keeping up and adjusting to change appropriately. Some of the women may want to stay in touch with the man of the family for reassurance and guidance until they get solid on their feet with their new lifestyle. That's all right.

He should allow them to keep in touch with him and even network if possible. The discussion of love and marriage may pop up between the man and any of his women. The most I can say is: that's between all of

The Epitome of a Player

you (things happen). The chapters about The Female Non Player and The Male Non Player will help tremendously in that area. The Gentleman of Leisure, Man of Leisure, and Lady of Leisure chapters will be additional help with love and marriage between male and female players. My intent is to lead you all in the right direction with the appropriate information that will help make the change bearable until you can get your program in order without help.

Now I need to help out our young men. I have decided not to leave them out. Those young players, who are walking around with your pants hanging about halfway down your rear end, with your underwear showing, should not look at that <u>mistake</u> as a hip style. There is not disrespect. I am simply saying that a true gentleman player will not allow his underwear to be showing while he is walking down the street. It's your choice.

This last definition for using power is about exercising control over others. You need to be in control of your own life before you can exercise control over anybody else's life. For that reason it will be a good idea for you young people to pull up your pants and <u>hope like hell</u> not too many people saw you carrying yourselves like that! Check and see if anybody is looking first. Ok, now pull those pants up. All right, that's good. Now don't you feel better? You are one step closer to the gentleman player.

Many of you young men are contemplating organizing a family of women to hit the streets and turn dates in order to bring you money. Well, I'm glad you're reading this book. In case you didn't catch on the first time, <u>read my lips</u>: The pimp and mack style has played out. It is out dated, molded, and ancient history. Flip the pages and catch up. <u>Advanced players</u> are working on a new chapter now. Read the Man of Leisure and the Gentlemen of Leisure chapters in this book again.

There was a wake up call a long time ago. Drugs and alcohol has played out. Narcotics were the biggest mistake in the game going all the way back to day one! Hustlers have been pulling off the streets by the boatloads and drying their systems out while living a life of abstinence from drugs. They have found their way back into the schoolrooms and are putting business proposals together.

In other words, the game has been elevated intellectually. This new academic system without drugs is becoming ever more popular all around the world. It is important that young people humble themselves, find a veteran in the game they respect, and get some advice on the <u>new styles of players</u>.

Players and Power

You don't even have to tag a player title on yourself. Read the Non Male Player chapter over again in order to deal with life with no titles tagged on you. It is simply a given fact that young people realize there is a new way of going about life rather than making the same mistakes their predecessor's made over the past years (some things go without saying).

There is a lack of control in many players that has become popular to the point of shamefulness. I'm talking about all those cool breezes that consider themselves to be players and hustlers whether they use drugs and alcohol, or they don't. This subject is about the child molester and rapist. I am not blind to the fact that many men who do this are people who have street knowledge and experience. They cultivated the ability to observe and manipulate others very well.

Back in 1976 I knew of a hustler in my hood that had done very well with women. The ladies gave him money, let him use their cars, ironed his clothes, cleaned his apartment; and would visit him in two's and three's. I was really taken back with his skills on handling women. His tactics were advanced and he was a classic example of a player displaying his power and control over women.

It pleased the ladies to serve his every need. They didn't mind giving their money and time to be part of his life. One day a hustler told me that this same player molested a little girl and did time in jail for it. My entire understanding became all messed up about players. What happened to his discipline with women?

I always admired him for his charisma and skills with the sexy women. I couldn't see the logic, the common sense, or the sanity behind him doing something very perverted like that. He had the savvy to have basically any nice looking lady he wanted. I have seen him pull many attractive women (and some ugly ones too).

My curiosity had got the best of me. One day I approached him, and just came out and asked him about the molestation. He just shrugged his shoulders with an obviously embarrassing grin, and said: I don't know. He couldn't even discuss it so I dropped the subject and made sure he would not be an associate of mines for too long. It was a case of abusive power, lack of control, and lust.

On the average, their husbands or their boyfriends in this country murder more than three women every year (per Presbyterian Church U.S.A., via internet Dec.2008). The number of killings in that area will largely decrease with implementation of my idea about having young kids

The Epitome of a Player

do role-playing on how to handle rejection (starting at age 11 or 12), and disputes in relationships. These classes can take place in grammar school, high school, college, and workshops.

It is an added insult to the game for players (and ex-players) to be climbing through the windows of many women, to rape them. They are also catching women on the streets and dragging them in a gangway, alley, bushes, park, or an abandoned building, to be molested. This is a classic example of the loss of discipline and misdirection caused by drugs, which in turn, created the many "hop along Cassidy, Joe Blow" imitator's; while they front in the game on a daily basis. I have thought about hustlers I have known who abused their street knowledge in the same form and fashion. Now it has come to light about a rise of men on the streets, considered to be players (who I didn't grow up with) who have done very well with women, but have made a decision to use their acquired street knowledge to force themselves on women.

When a man makes a bold decision to be a player; he has just chosen to exercise a great deal of control over his emotions and actions toward his women (or any other women). It is not easy for his ladies to have sex with him because that presents him as the average man, and how much money will he really make if he is his best customer?

A player is not the average man and his women are not looking for the average man. They will test him in the area of sex to see how strong and disciplined he is. Control over oneself in every area of life (including sex and drugs) presents a powerful asset to a player's personality. He has to master that control in order to be a professional in the game.

Many players do well until the inevitable happens. The family will fall apart at some point and time. Street hustling was never meant to be permanent. There are too many bad pitfalls for longevity. When the family breaks up for whatever the reason is, and everybody go their separate ways, the player didn't realize he would lose that strong self-discipline and control over women (and him).

A lot of panderer's are glad to give up that discipline because in actuality they really wanted to go to bed with their women more often. They couldn't, because the more they stayed in bed with their women the less money they brought in. He also would have been putting himself in a predicament to look like a weak man who is really a trick and not a real player. That's not cool.

Players and Power

Now we have the new player (or non player if he chose to leave out the title) with the new lifestyle whether he is drug free or not. He simply decided that it was time for a change. But now he doesn't have to keep his discipline anymore because he's not pimping or macking! That's why many of them end up going to bed with anything that comes their way with a skirt on after leaving the game. They have turned powerless over their emotions.

This loss of power has caused countless of them to observe women and manipulate them by climbing through their windows or pulling them in some gangway, alley, bushes, park, abandoned building (or wherever), and sexually molesting them. They are men who were never true players. They were wannabes, would have beens, could have beens, should have beens, and never will be's (the maybe is above that).

I spoke about the subconscious mind as being the infinite storage place for holding acquired knowledge and feeding that knowledge to the conscious mind as necessary. But without a balance in your life (mentally, physically, emotionally, and spiritually) the subconscious mind is not very effective in sending the necessary information to the conscious mind to help make that change easy. It is absolutely necessary for hustlers giving up their street life to store a good amount of spiritual knowledge into the subconscious mind so that it can feed the conscious mind information on humbleness and respect towards women.

It is important for streetwise hustlers to keep their discipline after giving up their street life. They need to do research on power and hold themselves accountable for looking at women in an entirely different way. Women are not sex objects waiting for some undisciplined man to climb through their window or drag them somewhere to satisfy his lust (and insanity). Women are human beings just like men and they deserve to be treated with the same respect that men expect from women. The rapist, and the molester, would not want some strange man doing the same thing to their daughters, mothers, sisters, or other female relatives of theirs. It is a privilege to live on the outside of a penitentiary in society. Street hustlers should conduct themselves with that manner and thought. Women deserve to walk down the street without fear and live in their homes without fear, just like men.

It is not only an abuse of power but also a defamation to force oneself on another individual without her consent. During the 1960's and 1970's you would seldom hear of someone raping or mugging a woman.

The Epitome of a Player

Respect needs to be restored to the streets and the game. Many hustlers who step out of the game should be aware of the control they need to maintain over themselves in order to have a meaningful relationship with others (especially women).

The incidents I just talked about were not meant to insult but to enlighten those who are unaware of the power within them. Power has to be controlled, respected, and never abused. The time is never too late to make a positive change. This message has touched some men in a spiritual way that has already caused them to look at women in a different way. Try out an exercise program. Finish your education and meditate for emotional control. Then get some help from someone with spiritual concepts, and in the process, stay focused on a meaningful and respectful relationship with just one woman (yeah, I know it's not easy, but it's safe; so try anyway).

13

WHY WOMEN CHOOSE PLAYERS

The scenario is about me sitting in my apartment dressed up casual with finger waves in my hair. I had my lid cocked ace duce to the side. The year was 1976 in Chicago and I had my money green 1974 LTD baby Brougham parked outside of my residence. I picked up the telephone and called one of my three ladies and said to her:

I'm about to come and pick you up and take you to the party in Park Forest Condominiums. You already know one of my other two girlfriends (I named her) that I'm picking up but you don't know the other one (I named her). I expect for all three of you to get along like sisters when you get in my car. I don't want any arguing, or misunderstandings, do you understand me? She said: "Yes."

I hung up the telephone and called my other two ladies up one at a time. I told them the same thing. They all agreed to conduct themselves like ladies. I picked each of them up and had one in the front seat and two in the back seat. I was not surprised when they socialized and got along as if they were sisters. I had them for a while and I educated them on my style, how they fit in my family, and how to conduct one another in this fast game. They were polite and cooperative. I was twenty-three years old at the time while living on 79th and Crandon on the Southeast Side of Chicago.

Now I would like to reflect back to a time when I was eighteen years old and I had been hanging out with my buddy (Eugene) who was eighteen. He put the first perm in my hair, showed me how to file my fingernails, and put the clear gloss fingernail polish on them. We wore fancy clothes (that were stolen), and then he and Rodney educated me on how to stand on the corner and socialize with the ladies as they walked by.

Eugene would let me sit by him while he called his women up to ask them for some money. I was learning the ropes. It took me from the age of eighteen to the age of twenty-one to get highly developed, but he was advanced at the age of sixteen (or sooner). I was astounded about his superior intellect with women at such a young age. We both lived on 79th and Crandon on the east side of Chicago at the time.

One day he told me about three of his women he was about to talk to. He said two of the ladies would meet him at this particular lounge

The Epitome of a Player

called The Ambassador; around 79th and Essex, and he was going to pick the other one up in his car. I rode in the back seat of his car and he had one of his girlfriends in the front seat as he drove to the Ambassador Lounge. When we went in he told the woman (who was in the front seat) to have a seat and he went up to the bar and sat in-between the two young ladies that was waiting for him. I said to myself: I would take any of his women because they were fine (with a capital F).

    His woman (sitting by me) waited patiently on my friend to finish talking to his other two girlfriends at the bar. I was about to go dance with some ladies, but I felt a little embarrassed leaving the young lady (who was a relative of mine) sitting at the table all by herself. So I sat there (too nice at the time), and kept her company. She wouldn't even dance with anybody. She just sat there waiting on my buddy. Talk about loyalty!

    After about an hour and a half went by, my buddy was still talking to the other two young ladies at the bar. He was acting like the one I was sitting with didn't exist. I said to her: Doesn't it bother you to sit here all this time waiting on (Eugene) my friend to get through talking to those other two young ladies. She said solemnly, "No, it doesn't bother me at all." This next example of a player interacting with his women is what made a believer out of me, in regards to their capabilities with the ladies.

    A few days after the occasion in the Ambassador lounge, I decided to visit a different buddy (in the same neighborhood) called "D." I hadn't seen him in a few weeks. I knocked on his apartment door and a lovely young lady with smooth coco brown skin and baby doll eyes opened the door. I asked her if my buddy was in and she said (coolly): "Yes."

    My buddy yelled from the back and said he was in the shower and to come to the back (I don't know what made him think I wanted to see him in the darn shower). When I came to the back, the young lady who answered the door was washing his body down with a face towel. There was another young lady with an appealing face and a brick house body-in the kitchen ironing his clothes to wear for that day (he was a big show off).

    He introduced me to both ladies and they were very polite and pleasant with their voices and demeanor. I could tell he had educated them very well on proper etiquette. In the back of my mind I said to myself: maybe I will try this out one day; and I did. But not with the three women

Why Women Choose Players

I mentioned at the beginning of this chapter. These were two separate occasions with different women. I had five different families of women before I stepped out of the mack game and elevated my style.

Now I will get to the point-which is the title of this chapter: Why Women Choose Players. I will tell you the <u>first</u> reason with one word: <u>Honesty</u>! I could probably stop there, but I will elaborate. That word means everything in the world to a woman in a relationship with a man. She would rather for a man to be up front about his lifestyle and what kind of relationship he wants with her. The men who have the problems are those who will hook up with a woman; and then sneaks around with other women.

The biggest mistake a man can make with a woman is to build up sincere feelings (on a one on one basis) between the two of them, and then she finds out he is seeing another woman. In many cases he will never be able to make it up to her. And if she does forgive him-the relationship will never be the same. There will always be something missing at that point. It would probably be best if he found another woman, but some men try to hang on thinking that things will return back to normal one day.

An experienced player understands that a woman has to be pleased emotionally before she can be pleased in any other way. Even sex doesn't mean anything to her until she is emotionally pleased with his personality. Looks help, but in the end, when it is all said and done-he needed to have established integrity and respect between the both of them. There is no such thing as a player cheating on a woman because she will meet all of his women (who are her wife in laws). And that takes me to the <u>second</u> reason on why women choose players.

<u>Audacity</u>! Just the fact that he had the nerve to mention two other women who are his-will build up enough intrigue in the women to want to get to know him better. Many women are use to having one man only and they are not accustomed to meeting a man who has the audacity to talk about his other women. Her meeting his other women is not the point at this stage. She will sit there in disbelief that he even said that, and she can see the look on the players face that this will be the last time she see him if she doesn't want to deal with his program. The woman typically says yes because of his audacity and the desire to see to believe.

After a woman decides that she wants to be a part of the player's life; an extreme curiosity builds up in her to see if this man is seriously the person he says he is. She was impressed with his honesty and now she can't wait to check out his audacity to introduce her to his other two women (or however many he has). She also want to check his ladies out and see how well behaved they are around her. And this brings me to the <u>third</u> reason on why women choose players.

<u>Follow up</u>! Having the audacity to mention his other women were one thing but having the boldness to follow through on what he said is another thing. He has presented a rare personality that she doesn't run into often and now she is impressed with his pursuit to do what he said he would do; and that's to introduce her to his other women.

Remember the conversation I had with my three ladies over the phone at the beginning of this chapter? When I picked up all three of them in my car I could see the admiration on their faces because I had the boldness to present myself to them all as a player; then <u>follow it up</u> by bringing all of them together in order to meet each other.

Women appreciate men who take care of business rather than just talking about it. Persistence is what makes things happen in this world. It doesn't even have to be in the area of accumulating women. For example: A banker would prefer that you do your homework before asking for a ten million dollar business loan. Don't just put the business proposal together any kind of way and then look for understanding.

Take your time and do the necessary research to find out what bankers are looking for in a business loan proposal. It takes anywhere from six months to two years to put a proficient business proposal together (depending on the type of business and what you will need).

The banker will need to see (at the end of the proposal) how much of your money you are willing to put down with the loan. Now you are in a predicament of trying to figure out how to come up with a reasonable amount of money to invest.

Do you give up at this point? Of course you don't give up. If you do not have the persistence to figure out how to come up with the money you need to go with the business loan-you will not have the persistence to run a business if you did get the loan.

Do you really think that you will run into any problems after getting the loan and then start putting the business together? You're darn right you will run into problems. The business is not going to run on its own. There will be products to buy like: Stationeries, pens, notebook paper, pencils, Xerox machines, a fax machine, computers, file cabinets,

Why Women Choose Players

desks, chairs, carpet, and a continuous supply that you didn't expect to need.

Then the dilemma of hiring personnel such as: A secretary, office workers, mangers, directors, and vice presidents quite constantly. You will also need a connection with a temporary agency in order to save money on overtime pay.

Let's not forget about the rental payment for the office space. Then there are the typical utility payments (gas, electric, and water). The cost of maintenance has to be included. Someone has to clean the area by moping the floors, cleaning desks, office machines, washing windows, repairing electrical problems, repairing the computers/office machines, painting, and maybe security.

You may include a cafeteria, depending on how big of a business you're putting together. If the business were starting out small, you would need to have an expansion plan in order to supplement your yearly gross income in order to make survival easier.

The expansion plan can be another office complex in another part of the city (like the south side instead of the north side). You may also decide to incorporate with another company and add new products and services to what you already have.

I went into extensive detail about what it takes to run a business because the player has to run his affairs the same way. The man of the family handles the money. He pays all the bills, buy the ladies clothes, buy the food (or send one of his women to the store with the money), and come up with a business plan for him and his family of women to manage, after life on the streets is over.

A woman has to see this type of business intellect evident in a man before she chooses into his family. Remember, the player is the employer of his women. He is running a business (even though it's illegal). He pays the money to get him or his women out of jail and hire an attorney for them if necessary. The business doesn't stop after the mack decides it's time to elevate his game to the man of leisure or gentleman of leisure.

His women will want to know what is next for their life. The ladies have the right to stick with him if they choose because the families of players' lives are a lifetime establishment. The gentleman of leisure (who was a mack) should already have the new business in progress.

It doesn't matter to his ladies if the new business is a string of beauty parlors, restaurants, barbershops, day care centers, grocery stores,

The Epitome of a Player

Laundromats, movie theaters. They simply want to stick with the family and adjust to the change. Those ladies in the family, who want to stick with the streets, have every right to do so, and still get with the new business at a later date if they desire.

This is exactly the reason why I have been suggesting in this book that young hustlers in this game who are trying to organize a family of women to be down for them; should seek the advice of a veteran in the game. He should also read over the man of leisure and gentleman of leisure styles (who don't use drugs, alcohol, or cigarettes). I realize that I'm redundant with that message, but I really need to be in order to get people to do their homework and make appropriate decisions in the fast lane.

Young people should not be disappointed about the pimp and mack styles being out of style. There are simply too many drugs, police force, jail time, graveyards, attorney payments, and overall failure, to save money and establish a legitimate business in that area. And if you did save money and establish a legitimate business, it would be appropriate at that point to determine why you still have a family of women (unless they enter the business with you)?

There is a business after the streets and <u>follow up is everything</u>. There are no ifs, buts, ands, or maybes, just be prepared to take care of your business appropriately or wait before you hit the streets. Don't sweat yourself or the game. It isn't worth it. Don't get caught up with the egotism of having multiple women down for you in the game. It's all about doing what works in life. Make your business work and remember: Patience is a virtue.

The <u>fourth reason</u> on why women choose players is because of their <u>intellect</u>. Remember what I said about education never coming to a cease? Education is found in many different forms, fashions, and places. Experienced players continue to educate themselves in all areas of life. I have named many of the areas that they endeavor in, such as: real estate sales and real estate investments, stocks, bonds, computers, assertiveness, tact, etiquette skills, salesmanship; partnerships, mastermind groups, lots of reading, seminars, and workshops.

I could have named more areas, but I'll let the interested party do the rest of the work; the experienced player is advanced in knowledge and the appropriate application of that knowledge when putting legitimate projects together and making the money fall. That's what we are about and that's what we do.

If a woman is in a players family and she is not becoming more intelligent through educational programs on a yearly basis then she is with the wrong person. Even if she just picks up the habit of reading a lot of self help-material-she is learning and advancing in the game. How can the ladies engage in a legitimate business after leaving the streets if they are not staying educated?

This is not good news for the hustlers that (dropped out of high school) hit the streets to make fast cash because they don't like to go to school and do homework. They don't even like to read books. There is a big misunderstanding about street hustle. The game is for intellectuals and not the illiterate wannabes who are simply in everybody's way. The legit businesses that I described earlier about putting proposals together-was an example of the intelligence the player is expected to have.

A woman is a reflection of her man and vise versa. If you run into a well-disciplined woman with intellect, then check out her man. If you run into a man who is well disciplined with intellect, then check out his woman. They both compliment each other.

There is no faking in the game. A man can get by for a while with a good conversation, nice clothes to wear, and a nice car. That's enough to pull a couple of women in your corner that will be down for you. But how long can the man get away with the fact that he only has an education that's equal to a sophomore in high school (or lower)?

At some point and time a player's women will wise up to the fact that their man was strong enough to get the family started, but now he is feeling his way through the game. The main reason many players hang on to women for a while is because the ladies didn't know much about the game themselves. They were guessing and feeling their way through the game when they chose him because of his materialistic flash.

The game has never been about drugs, jails, and failure. It has always been about success, material possessions, and a higher level of thinking, which in actuality, is introduced to them by the player. So he has to do his homework and make sure he is prepared to bring success, maturity and advancement to the family. That's his job and it is absolutely necessary that he do it well.

The <u>fifth</u> reason why women choose players is because of their <u>discipline.</u> A woman truly appreciates a man who can control his need for physical pleasure; but she doesn't need him if he conducts himself like the average savage man that last ten seconds in the sex act. Then he rolls over and starts snoring (loudly) in his sleep while the woman is unsatisfied and disgusted

A player is not the average man. An attractive woman knows that she can find a man anywhere who will try to keep her in bed. The average man's thinking is so corrupt with lust he will skip the foreplay and take the entire thrill, excitement, anticipation, and the sensuality out of the act of love. The point of boredom reaches the woman at that point.

She will be able to tell him how often he will want sex each day, what times of the day he will want it and how long he will last (which is not long because he will only be thinking about his own climax as he simply rolls over on his back with self gratification).

That's what happens in the long run in typical relationships. The man becomes complacent with lust and the woman becomes emotional with need. This is far from the case in a family of women with a well-disciplined man. In that scenario, the women will be making the advances towards the player in regards to when he will please them sexually. He has already done an excellent job of establishing intrigue, fascination, desire; and the right mood for the right time. It is very important for him not to let his physical feelings control his mind.

It should be understood that the typical woman would take money over sex. The cordial relationship on up to marriage is for companionship more so than love. This is where the player comes in at, because women know that money comes before feelings with him. They don't have to worry about him being all over them with uncontrollable lust while the bills are overdue and her man (or husband) doesn't have a job.

The thrill was gone a long time ago (in the prior relationship I just described). But that's never the case with the mature, accountable, player. His women never know what to expect because he keeps them guessing in order to keep the intrigue going between them. Discipline doesn't come overnight. It has to be practiced. This following poem is a good example of the discipline between a player and his woman:

Why Women Choose Players

TEST DATE

So true to the test
I say lets choose
Maybe it's my figure
that make emotions flow
As there will be a date
when the entire sum
will need to be balanced
Because one to its equation
would hope to be an addition
of what would be harmonious
Just to come down to two
But will there be
such a simple summary
turned out to be intricate
to make a rationale
As I look at the calendar
and the ax's
outweigh the oh's
To my marvelous indignation
I suggest that it's time
So why should I wait
until the end of each
and every month
To the very last day
as you well know
Only three hundred
and sixty five
All the way down
to the last second
You came
And I said
Oh!

By Ernest Ivy II

It was not about the act itself, but the strong mental and intuitive projection of the act that made the ecstasy worth waiting for. This is a scenario that the player will create and instill in her mind month after month, year after year. There is never such a thing as complacency. She will always think about it, want it, need it; and can't wait for it. He will wait until that final moment of intense delight.

I truly believe that many readers will not pick up on the fact-the man and woman in that poem was in the act of making love. From the start it seemed as if she was waiting for him to come over. But how could he have reached his climax at the end of the poem where it states: <u>you came</u> (if he wasn't there)?

The expressions from the woman's thoughts from the beginning to the end of the poem were typical of the impression that players put on their women. This particular woman is very attractive and use to getting her way with men-except the one she was making love to. Her thoughts were on the personal feelings she was having about not getting her way and having to wait for sex when she was ready for it. The true players should never give their women sexual pleasure when she or he is ready. The act of love should only take place when he feels that the time and place is appropriate with the mood and not just the mood by itself. It is the act of a professional.

I will admit that the average man typically has that kind of discipline and patience when he first starts out in a relationship with a woman. But after a short period of time (one to two years or less) he loses that discipline. The woman eventually becomes a sex machine to jump up and down on. Then he rolls over on his back like a lazy swine and starts mumbling in his sleep. It doesn't matter anymore if the woman reached a climax or not. He has turned into a pig. The cuddling, small kisses and small talk, is past history now. The good for nothing slob doesn't care anymore. He has her.

The <u>gentleman player</u> knows better than that. He realizes there's never a time when he can say <u>I got her</u>. A man can always lose his woman or wife. He has her so long as he maintains the discipline he had when he first met her. In the case of players who are receiving money from women, it is vital that they maintain their discipline. That's one of the reasons why she chose him. She is not looking for the average love affair with the average man. Even if they have been together for two years, he always looks at the relationship as if he just met her. Each and every moment is still special. He is still flamboyant and still has that ignite in his kiss with that sensuous touch as he embraces her. He is still intriguing and gracious with the roses, violets, candy, gifts, surprise dinners, and special-nonstop uniqueness in the act of his love. He knows to be sensitive while holding her close and using sincere words after the climax. The finishing stage has to produce longevity of the love process.

The <u>sixth</u> reason why women choose players is because they're expecting effectiveness <u>in money management.</u> There are many women throughout the world who prefer that the man handle all the money and

Why Women Choose Players

bills. And that's fine. Somebody has to do it. Many men do well in this area, but the irony is that the same men don't realize their management job goes farther than just money.

It is the player's responsibility to manage drug use in the family. The best solution would be abstinence, but that's not likely with the pimp and mack style; because drugs, alcohol and cigarettes, go with the territory in that circle. That's why popularity of those styles is fading quickly. Not only have their women been getting strung out, but their men also. Many of them (the man or woman) overdose or end up doing time because of a bad judgment due to drug and alcohol use.

For those players who have not elevated their style to the man of leisure or the gentleman of leisure, and are still playing the street games; it is imperative for you to know that it is your job to keep your women and yourselves from over doing it with narcotics. It would be appropriate to get educated by a veteran in the game if you have not done so. You also need to realize that your street style was either never meant to be, or it is temporary.

Too many of us jumped out the plane and forgot the parachute. We hit the streets without all the information needed to make precise choices. We were gung-ho. You jump in the game, do what you need to do and pull out! It was never meant to be a career or amusement parks with plenty of whoopee do fun, sex and drugs; every single day. That type of fantasy is not called pimping and macking. That's called being strung out on drugs, lust, and a zip fools world.

This is your wake up call. Make a change and lead your women in the right direction. Drugs and alcohol have played out in the game. It was never necessary for success in the first place. Too many hustlers have been misinformed and mislead. That confusion has lead to a lack of judgment. Read over: The Man of Leisure, The Gentleman of Leisure, and The Lady of Leisure chapters; then make some quick decisions to correct those past, crazy mistakes. It's never too late to escape from madness.

The <u>seventh</u> reason why women choose players is because they want to <u>belong to a family</u> <u>that shares the same interest they do in life</u>. Many women don't prefer the routine system of a 9 to 5 job. They find the life on the streets to be more intriguing and challenging. It is a <u>way of life</u> for them. There are many people who will not give up drugs and street life no matter what a book says or no matter who express the dangers of that lifestyle to them.

The Epitome of a Player

The ability to change is not easy. Change is not an overnight process. But at the same token there are many people who adjust to logic very well. Many people won't mind giving up the streets and drugs once they realize there is a better system for acquiring the wealth and success they want out of life. This book is for those people who are able to change, and for those who find change difficult, but will try anyway.

The <u>eighth</u> reason why women choose players is because of <u>intrigue</u>. Many women have read pimp books and watched pimp movies. The lifestyle of players at that point became mentally stimulating to them. It presented a challenge for many people to live out their fantasies. I have socialized with many players who have obtained educational degrees and can mesmerize women with just their conversation.

There are many men who look like the wolf man, but can talk like Romeo. All a woman need to do is entertain the thought-then run into the man who presents the dialogue and lifestyle similar to what she has read in books and seen in movies. Then the stage has been set with her being the new star in the man's family.

There is an old saying that curiosity killed the cat. It has done the same with many women when matters have gotten crazy after they entered street life. Numerous women find out too late that the players who wrote those pimp books are advanced in the game and will not be found on the streets. And the men they see in the movies portraying a player are actors who are making a boatload of money for their role.

I am suggesting that the women, who have suffered in a player's family; read over the chapters titled: Wannabes-Would Have Beens-Could Have Beens-Should Have Beens-Never Will Be's-and-Maybes. After reading those chapters over again they will realize that they never had a real player in the game, but simply someone who had enough of a player's characteristics to fool not only her, but many other women also. It will be appropriate for those women who have survived the terrifying nightmare of being in such an atrocious family-to read over the Lady of Leisure chapter again and make better choices with their lives.

The <u>ninth</u> reason why women choose players is because <u>they didn't have anywhere else to go</u>. He provided shelter, food, and hope for her. Many women come from broken homes and poor communication with either one or both parents. The bad communication may be; because of the females drug use. It really isn't a good idea for parent's to overreact when they soon find out (and many parents will experience this if they already

Why Women Choose Players

haven't) that their daughters <u>swim</u> and <u>bathe</u> in drugs and alcohol. If they give their kids a hard time about it-they can easily end up in the pimp or macks family.

Parents should remember that it was not easy for them to avoid drugs and alcohol, and many of them <u>swam</u> and <u>bathed</u> in the substances themselves.

It is highly unreasonable to expect a great deal of maturity and effective decision making from teenagers because they have not lived in the world long enough for that. Even those young people who are in college getting that exceptional education will be curious about marijuana and alcohol. Many of them try it out.

Parents need to be above abusive language and lack of empathy and understanding with their kids. Someone on the streets will give them the understanding that you didn't give them, and that could be dangerous. It takes humbleness and the acceptance of humility to make it in life. That saying goes for the parents and their kids. It would be wise for parents to have spiritual balance in their lives so they can be down to earth with their children. Don't just put them down. Try to relate to them and remember your wild party days before becoming a parent.

The <u>tenth</u> (and last) reason women choose players is because <u>he is their idea of the man they want to marry</u>. That's right! Believe it or not <u>it is true</u> that many women pick out the worst man for them because he is interesting.

There are women who are professional busters. They will go along with everything that the player says and then do their best to get into arguments with the other women in the family for the purpose of running them off. And if she can't run all of them off, she will just hang in there through thick and thin until the other women leave for various other reasons.

Some women leave because the player is physically abusive. Some of the ladies will choose into some other player's family, because he had established a better conversation and better living arrangement than her last man. Some women leave because they eventually realize the lifestyle in the fast lane is not as glamorous as it seemed. But that one woman who is determined to hang in there through the rain, snow, sleet and hail; will not go anywhere. She has found her dream husband and in many cases a woman of that nature does end up marrying him. It happens because he admires her dedication and toughness in a difficult lifestyle. Now that's what I call a happy ending.

14

WHY MEN BECOME PLAYERS

In order for you to be the epitome of a player it will be essential to understand where you came from, where you're at, why you're there and where you're headed. In other words, there has got to be common sense to your existence and meaning to the choices you make in life. This will sum up the rationality of why you became a player.

I am going to break down the appropriate reasons, complications, and appropriate adjustments to a man's ultimate choice of living a player's lifestyle. It is very important that the young hustlers develop a constructive vision out of what I'm about to say. Then start the process of making a reality out of those thoughts. As I said before, there should be a happy ending to all a person puts himself through on the streets.

The scenario starts: Ogden Park in Chicago; on the Southwest side at 63rd and Elizabeth. It was about 9pm and I was standing by the park with three of my buddies. It was 1967 and I was fourteen years old. The homeboys were talking about a gentleman who lived with his mother. He didn't have a car and he had three women who were down for him in the game. The ladies would go back and fourth to his crib (house) bringing him money. Then they go right back to the streets. I never heard of a man having women in that capacity.

I didn't even have a girlfriend at the time. But here was a young man about 21 year's old living with his mother and he didn't even have a car. He had three women bringing him money. I was dumbfounded. It was a conversation that I could not elaborate on so I stood there listening while my thoughts would roam. I had flashes of me with several women in my car as I drove along, knowing that they were all mines.

And there you have it. The thought is the cause of it all. At some point and time many men have had a similar experience. It doesn't really matter how those thoughts came to them. It's the entertainment of those thoughts that will eventually form the man into the player. If you don't entertain the thought then you don't entertain the deed. I came from an area where everything was basically discussion. We had not gotten started with our careers. I never thought much of that conversation after that day. I didn't think it would ever be a reality in my life.

The Epitome of a Player

I had already started smoking marijuana, cigarettes, and drinking alcohol at the age of fourteen. I didn't comprehend at the time that I was entertaining the thought. I also didn't know that pimping was in my blood because when I was twenty-one years old my uncles had told me that my father was a pimp and a gangster. It was too late by that time because I had three women, a money green 1974 LTD baby Brougham (in 1974), and a pocket full of money everyday. I was a young mack. My father was never around so I could only take my uncles word about what he was about. It didn't really matter because I had my life to live and obviously, I couldn't live his.

My mother moved to the Southeast side on 79th and Crandon in Chicago in 1968. I was fifteen years old. By the time I was sixteen I had met two friends on the same block who had me standing on the corner of 79th and Crandon with them. They were teaching me how to socialize with the young ladies as they walked by. I was taught what to say, how to say it, and when to say it. In a matter of two to three weeks I was telling the ladies that I was a professional as I stacked up on phone numbers.

One of my buddies put butter (perm) in my hair for the first time. Curly Afros were in style during that time. I was taught the correct way of filing my fingernails to make them grow long, and how to put the clear gloss on my nails to make them shine. Our nails looked so good that many young ladies would hide their hands behind their back when we came around them, because our nails looked better than theirs. We actually gave many women tips on how to grow their nails.

We were starting to feel real cool, calm, and collected, with our confidence riding on a high. We felt that we were able to pull just about any woman we wanted. Little did I know that there was a point to all this (make the money and pull out), and none of us ever got that point right; even though we all knew what our destination was supposed to be like? The mess had not hit the fan yet.

We were still in the beginning stages of preparation for the real issue. But I hadn't realized it. I was having too much of a good time. I had learned how to go over my scripts for conversations with the ladies before I came outside. We would all meet in front of our residences. Then we would check each other over to make sure that everyone's hair was neat, clothes were clean, and well pressed. Our entire body had to smell fresh and be clean. Our shoes had to be shined and we all had to pull out a pen

Why Men Become Players

with blank paper to show that we were prepared to write down the ladies phone numbers.

If any of our attire were not in order, we had to go back home and straighten out the problem. If someone's shoes were not shined he had to go back home and shine them. If somebody left his pen and paper, he had to go back home and get it. If a person's hair was not well groomed-he had to go back in the house and groom his hair. Everybody else would proceed to go to the corner and start getting phone numbers because they were in order. The person (or person's) that had to go back home went through another inspection from the homeboys when he eventually came to the corner where everybody was standing. We had ourselves under very strict discipline by the time we were seventeen. We were young professionals.

I have just laid out the circumstances of where I came from (the Southwest side of Chicago) all the way to the point of where I was at by the age of seventeen. This is a typical scene of how the average teenagers get started on the road to being young players. It starts out slow and then it gets to be a cool game to play.

We practiced our dance steps in our parent's basements with two or three women. Everybody in our area could step well. Around that time a couple of young men had borrowed a bunch of nice looking clothes out of a clothing business and forgot to return them. Behind that incident my buddies and I had more than enough fancy clothes to wear everyday. We dressed much better than the average kid our age. The marijuana, alcohol and cigarettes, went along with the game, because we had no knowledge about any other style except the pimp and mack. Some of us read material on the gentleman of leisure but it was on the street style only. It was all about being cool, smooth and too good to be true. We all thought we were "the hit of the year."

Many young people can relate to what I'm talking about in this chapter because many of you are coming up the same way around the same age we were at (when seventeen). It's alright for young persons to understand why they chose to be young players, so long as you know what your destination is suppose to be, and how to apply those techniques. The only way that young hustler's who are already out on the streets can be the epitome of a player, is to make the appropriate adjustments that come with the territory. That's what I'm about to talk about now.

The most experienced young player in our group stated that we were suppose to make our money fast, pull off the streets, and make some

The Epitome of a Player

legitimate investments. And that was it. There was no mention of what investments we should make or how to go about doing it; which presented a problem. We got stuck on cool.

By the time everyone was twenty-one years of age we had at least three women or more riding in our cars with us. They put cash in our pockets and did whatever we asked them to do. We accomplished what we were trained to do.

Everybody was so elated with going to the parties; having their women by their side, stepping, hanging out in the pool rooms, the bars, lounges, kicking it with other players in different cities; while none of us was working a 9 to 5 job. We quit our jobs because we were hustling well and everybody kept a fat bankroll in their pockets. We were in the mix. We ate well, slept good, dressed well, had plenty of sex, and did whatever the heck we wanted to do. We actually thought we had accomplished the American dream.

I have just explained to the readers why men become players; for the power, prestige, freedom, and the good times. But we blew it! That's right! Everybody blew it big time. At some point and time everybody was supposed to be pulling off the streets to use their money and intellect to make investments. We were going to start our own legitimate businesses, but we got hooked on drugs.

We were unprepared for our drug addition that led us to crime, car accidents, penitentiary time, and death for many of my peers. My women would tell me that I had it all together. They said I had them, money, a nice car, and nice clothes with a nice crib (apartment); and intellect. They told me that all I had to do was slow down on the drugs. They felt that I was getting too high and they were right.

My buddies and I had egos the size of the United States. You could put the facts to us but we wouldn't comprehend plain sense. It wasn't until I reached my forties and started trying to help younger people out-that I was able to see myself-at their age (their teens and twenties). I may as well be talking to "the hand."

It is difficult for me to lead young people in the right direction-especially if they are on the streets doing drugs and got a few women in their corner. That's why I decided to put the information in a book. I can reach out to more of them through a book by getting more subjects and information to them.

Why Men Become Players

There is nothing wrong with being cool, hip, and in the mix. I am simply adding information to the player's game that young people play, so they can rise above negative circumstances. Hopefully the information I'm giving will help them be a better man and player in the game.

I have just identified my teenage years with those of many young people today. I have also empathized with many of the players in the game right now that's making money and getting high. They are on cloud nine with a few women in their corner. Now I am going to list ten questions for the young players to answer to themselves so they can be ready to elevate their game to a higher level.

1. Did you realize that hustlers on the street were supposed to make their money fast then pull out of the game and invest in a business venture?

2. Are you prepared to pull out of the game and use your acquired street knowledge to decide what business venture you will invest your time into if you don't make the money on the streets you expected to make? Every hustler will not do well financially on the streets so it will be wise to pull out of the game with your life if you're that close to losing it. Then simply: continue your education in some kind of school program and add that knowledge to what you already know.

3. Will it bother you to join a book club, go to the library and go to seminars? Try reading magazines and newspapers in order to add more knowledge to your school program. Your street knowledge and your self education program will help you out a great deal in regards to being the independent contractor or the entrepreneur that you were meant to be.

4. Did you realize that the illegal activities you young players participate in are really done because you are strongly motivated to work independently of any kind of employer? Many hustlers don't like taking orders so street hustle provides an out for them to call their own shots while making money their way. They can go to a school and talk to a counselor about how to get started in a self-employed business. This will take hard work and study, but it will

The Epitome of a Player

be a good investment of their time-without the risks involved on the streets. Besides, that is the destination of the player anyway. You might as well get started with your education off the streets now. You simply needed someone to tell you that it's the right thing to do and now is the best time to do it.

5. If you are a player on the streets with women in your family; are you prepared to talk to your ladies to help them decide on a positive direction to go in if you decide it's best to break up the family and allow everyone to elevate their game? Many men don't care about their women when they are ready for a change; which is sad because the women are the backbone and the bulk load of the money in the players' family and everyone should benefit. It was never meant to be a hustle where as the man get paid, leave when he get ready, forget the women who may be having drug problems and can't go home to her blood relatives. I am saying this because the publication of this book will have many people on the streets thinking about the appropriate move to make. A lot of you players have already been thinking about making a change before reading this book. Be mature and responsible by not making a rush move if you have women living with you. Everybody will need a place to stay so work things out like the intellectual man that you are.

6. If you are in the penitentiary and are about to be released back into society within several months on up to a year-are you prepared to elevate yourself in the game with the man of leisure or gentleman of leisure styles without the use of drugs and alcohol? The use of drugs and alcohol was involved in the lives of many incarcerated inmates. It would seriously be ill advised to make the same mistake again. You can choose not to tag a title on yourself at all (read the male non player chapter again). Change is necessary for success at this stage of the game for you. Copies of this book will reach many people who are locked up. This is a good time to think about the contents of this material.

7. Do you mind confiding in a friend or relative for assistance? Sometimes it's not easy for a man (who has relied on the streets to make a living) to change his ways and go back to school-then work

on an honest job until he can justly, establish his own business. Sometimes he will need the help of a person who is close to him that he can depend on for good sound advice. I suggest that many hustlers slow down and take their time to make a sound decision over the next few days with the help and guidance of a trusted friend. This book is the turning point in many people's lives that were missing the knowledge they needed to make some positive choices and move on with their lives. Humble yourself and ask for help. You'll be glad you did.

8. Did you know that many ex-cons end up right back in jail less than a year after being released? There will be many people reading this book who have been out of the penitentiary for less than a year. I am suggesting that you get some readjustment counseling to fit back into society-without engaging in a crime that could send you back to the joint. And you know darn well you don't want to go back there, so don't put yourself in that position. It is not the prison official's job to tell you to get readjustment counseling. Safer foundation (312-922-2200) does an exceptional job of helping ex-cons find jobs and re-adjust back into society. Give them a call and find out what area's they can help you with.

9. Is it difficult for you to save money? Many hustlers find it hard to save money because they love buying clothes, cologne, jewelry, shoes and narcotics. To be a successful businessman you will need the ability to budget and save money. Even if you save ten dollars a month to start out with-it's ok. Just try getting use to saving something every month and then increase your savings amount periodically.

10. Can you humble yourself and start spending money and time with your children if you haven't been doing it? Many men would be surprised at how depressed and lonely children feel when they know that they have a father who doesn't come around. Children feel that something is wrong with them and that's why their father doesn't come around. It's ok if you are mad at the kid's mother. People have misunderstandings, but don't stay mad at her year after year. Talk to someone about spiritual concepts that can help

you humble yourself and make up with the children's mother. Then you can spend time with your children. Our kids are a gift and a blessing to us. You will be blessed abundantly for spending time and love with your children.

Those ten questions are enough for a street hustler to think about, and hopefully make the appropriate adjustments in order to have a positive destination in life. That's something my friends and I did not have when I was a teenager. We knew the right thing to do at some point and time but we didn't have the knowledge or the guidance of a mature adult or veteran who could put everything in an appropriate perspective. That would have helped us understand how to make those changes work.

It is good to know why you do something; so that you can predict the outcome; and then you make things happen. I have explained why men typically become players. I have provided the most reasonable outcomes and the systems for making that happen. I will not leave you hanging with only the previous ten questions I just asked you. The next two chapters (Making Things Happen and The Psychology of a Players Circle) will give you additional knowledge, techniques, and methods to help you be the successful person you were meant to be in life.

15

MAKING THINGS HAPPEN

In this chapter and the next, I will tell you what to do, how to do it, and when to do it. I will move you. There will be no excuse for not having a positive direction in life-along with the remedy for making your dreams come true after reading this chapter and the next. You will not be able to sit still behind these ideas and techniques that will change your life forever and it will be for the best.

Everybody has player characteristics in him or her, and that's to a certain degree; because this world calls for a very important game plan for survival. A person can manipulate a given system without doing anything illegal. It is fundamentally a matter of salesmanship when it comes around to giving someone what he or she is looking for in order to get what you want. All I need to know is a little bit about you so that I can give you what you want. I will also tell you a little bit about me with hopes that you may be able to give me what I want.

There are several definitions of manipulate. This is the definition I have chose to pick out, and will use for this topic: <u>To control or operate by skilled use of the hands</u>. I am about to give you plenty of ideals for obtaining what you want out of life by using your hands and skills. The word skills represent the use of the mind to control the hands for jotting down and then analyzing ideas for implementation of projects that will be successful enough to produce financial gain.

In other words, the hands can be used for all the wrong purposes or for all the right purposes. I am going to re-direct your thoughts if you have been using your hands to pick up guns, drugs, alcohol and cigarettes. Start picking up the ink pen with your hands. Only pick up what you need and keep your hands away from anything you don't need. You control your hands. Nobody can control them for you. I am directing your hands to be used for the right purposes and the mind will take over from there.

The main principles to stay focused on are production and financial gain. The ideas that I give you are designed for motivation and purpose for stimulating your subconscious to produce the thoughts to your conscious mind that will enable you to innovate and then initiate your own unique ideas for production and gain. Your hands will need to pick up a pen and paper for this project. You don't need to pick up anything else.

The Epitome of a Player

Write at the top of your paper: <u>Make It Happen</u>! This will be the beginning of an absolutely new way of thinking. I have never been content with the terms called goals and mission statement. Those terms make me feel as if I'm setting out to accomplish something at some point and time that I designate in the future. I consider that process to be just a little bit too sluggish in a very fast pace economy that's dominated by downsizing, empowerment and facilitation.

Why set out to accomplish something that can happen right now? If a supervisor gives you a project to do in a certain amount of time-it will be inappropriate to explain the problems to him at a later date on why you couldn't get the job done. Your supervisor doesn't want to hear that. He wants results. You needed the confidence to know right then and there that you could <u>make it happen</u>.

There should have been no doubt in your mind. You see; it's not the process that makes things happen; it's the confidence in your skills that lets you know right then and there, that the project will happen before the process even start. All you need to do is use the system I am giving you in this chapter and the next (The Psychology of a Players Circle).

After writing <u>Make It Happen</u> at the top of your paper, write under it, five different ways to make money legally. Do not write down any ideas that you do not feel can be accomplished by you even before the process starts. This system is about positivism and success-not doubt and failure.

In other words-you know that you will <u>make it happen!</u> The process is not the important part. This will prepare you for these other ideas. I will give you some examples in order to help you create some ideas of your own. You could write a book. Many people who have been on the streets hustling have plenty of knowledge they can share with people all around the world in a book. They can simply pick out an area that people need help in or entertainment in, and write about it.

Many publishing companies are looking for new writers with unique writing styles. Children's books, real life stories, horror, action stories and love stories are very popular subjects with publishers and the audiences they cater to. You can also rent an office or store front building and use it for a typing service, selling wholesale products at retail price, a Laundromat, a game room, a pool room, a party hall, a cake and pastry service, a professional counseling service, a day care, a roller skating rink, a tax preparation service, an investment service or a store selling books,

Making Things Happen

newspapers and magazines, that have a game room on the other side. That should be enough tips to get you thinking of some good, fresh ideas of your own, or you can use one of my ideas for now.

Write down what you would like to be doing one year from now, three years from now, five years from now, and ten years from now. You can look at the list of ideas that you wrote down-in order to help you out with this one. You will need to acknowledge that what you put down on paper will definitely happen (otherwise don't jot it down).

Don't try to figure out all the angles on how it will happen right now because I still have more ideas ahead. You will understand how you will make it happen after that process is over with. The words <u>make it happen</u> are action words that are much stronger than the words-goals and mission statement (which are words that's been around for quite awhile anyway). You will be surprised at the ideas that your subconscious mind will send out to your conscience mind because of these new techniques and information that I am providing in this book.

Change is a strong power source. Whenever circumstances become different-the subconscious has to kick out different information. You have several new ideas of your own roaming through your mind about unique ways of putting different businesses together.

Some of you feel like picking up the phone right now and calling up some friends to see if they want to be a business partner with you. It may be a good idea to get together with two more people; then your five ideas-together with all of their five ideas-would make fifteen ideas. Now you have a partnership to work with so that you won't have to figure out everything by yourself. Sounds pretty good huh? That's cool.

Put this book down for a few minutes and write those ideas down on your make it happen sheet. Now, just pick up the telephone and make it happen right now by arranging a date, time, and place for everyone to meet and then discuss the partnership. Make sure everyone bring his or her five ideas. You have just created a business. <u>It will happen</u>. There will be no such thing as excuses later on about why it did not work out. I will give you all the input you need to be successful.

If you designate a partnership between three and five people, it would be an excellent idea to designate responsibilities according to the different skills each partner possess. One person may be good at writing a business proposal for the lending institution. Another person may be good at writing out the partnership agreement form. The <u>stationary stores</u> have

The Epitome of a Player

<u>partnership agreement forms</u>. You can elect to choose three different kinds to look over and then structure your own form from those you have picked out. Or you can choose one of the three samples if you are in agreement with what you read in one of them.

Try picking out people who have pretty good credit. Everyone can look up the three different credit agencies on the Internet and order their credit report from each agency in order to see if anything needs to be cleared on your credit report. Somebody in your group will probably be knowledgeable about clearing up your credit. The lending institution may want to know how much of your money you will put up in order to get the loan (unless your credit is superior). For that reason it will be necessary to collect a reasonable amount of dues each month to be applied towards the necessary down payment with any of the other expenses that may come up before you get the loan (and you will definitely make the loan happen).

You will need some dependable people in the partnership who will show up on time at your designated meetings to discuss the business. One or two meetings a month is appropriate. There is no turning back. This is not a business venture for the weak, weary, and easily discouraged person. This is for the strong, assertive and positive person who doesn't give up in life.

And don't act like the business will be a success once you get the business loan. The business venture became a success when you picked up the telephone and made the arrangements to meet with several people to put the project in progress! You are already successful. It will happen! Keep the words <u>make it happen</u> roaming through your thoughts. You have to make it happen and you <u>will</u> make it happen!

Many people believe in tithing so they can organize a spiritual partnership between three and five people (or however many they choose). The partners in this group would have to put an emphasis on this non-stop tithing with strong expectations of a blessing. But even in that situation everybody will still need to do his or her part to <u>make it happen</u>.

I don't want to leave out the teens and young adults who are not using drugs or alcohol (those teens and young adults who are using drugs and alcohol should get to a drug treatment center; because narcotics have been a negative affect on creativity and they destroy relationships).

When I was a teenager I was part of a social club with my teen peers on the block where I lived. We had members from the surrounding areas also. We called ourselves the Afro Knights Social Club (sometimes

Making Things Happen

we had to explain to people that we were not a gang). We knocked on the doors of our neighbors and told them that we had started a social club and wanted to know if our club members could use their homes, apartments and basements, in order to carry out our meetings and parties. We said that there would be no drugs or alcohol allowed.

The neighbors knew us very well and were excited about opening up their residences to us. They even invited us to their block club meetings and we came. The adults and parents were really proud of what we were doing. Our social club established different positions such as: president, vice president, treasurer, spokesman, and negotiators to help us find more residences that could be used by us for meetings and parties. We collected monthly dues from all the members for the use of buying pop and potato chips. We had a door charge of two or three dollars. We sold the pop and the chips were free.

This would be a good idea for teenagers and a very good learning experience to improve their responsibilities, and maturity when interacting with adults and parents. This would also put them in the business frame of mind for starting their own business someday. They could keep the money in a bank account and find out how to balance their own checkbook. Every experience that the teenagers learn in the business world will help them in some form or fashion later on in life.

Remember that I'm listing these ideas to help stimulate your subconscious mind to release new ideas to your conscious mind that you were not aware of. At this point and time, many people should have jotted down at least 5 to10 unique ideas of their own. Don't stop writing. The more ideas the better; and jotting down at least 5 ideas was to at least get you started.

Here is an idea that could be used by the teen social club or older adults: A home based business can be established for cutting and watering home owners grass, shoveling their snow, cleaning-vacuuming people's homes, cleaning-vacuuming offices, taking donations of unwanted clothes and furniture from neighbors-then hold a garage sale. You could also put your unwanted furniture and clothes with the garage sale. Try advertising in the newspapers for donations of furniture and clothes; then tell the donators that 20% will go to charity, and the other money will be used for business expenses and salaries (or come up with your own reasons). A safe baby-sitting service could also be included. When enough money has been made the members could rent office space and work from there.

The Epitome of a Player

Many people should be jotting down ideas on their <u>make it happen</u> sheet. Start on another page after filling up one page. This is a system that calls for jotting down ideas as they come to you. Start keeping a pen and paper with you in order to jot down ideas wherever you are at-when the ideas come to you.

I represented a buyer once when I was working out of a real estate office as a real estate broker and the buyer bought a HUD home for 18,000 dollars. The market value for that area was 50,000-so he made a 32,000 profit off the deal. He made a decision to rent the house out instead of selling it-so he will have more than a profit of 32,000 when he decides to sell it. He told me that he learned that technique from a $60.00 dollar tape. The point, which I'm basically making, is that: it's appropriate, sensible and highly beneficial to look into all avenues of investing; including real estate. Don't leave one stone unturned when it comes around to doing your homework. Millionaires and billionaires have gone through the same hustle and bustle (with some having the silver spoon), and got started in real estate. But they had to learn from the professionals first. That's why I just told the story about the young man paying $60.00 dollars for a tape on foreclosures. Many people don't believe in those books and tapes, but they work if you will work. <u>Make it happen</u>.

That's one of the new thoughts I want to instill in the readers minds-<u>make it happen</u>-then get use to thinking that way, because you will not wait on circumstances, fate, or luck to favor you when you're in the make it happen frame of mind. <u>You can make it happen</u>!

Many people keep buying books and tapes until they either get enough information, courage, or both, in regards to buying property. They will have many books and tapes sitting in a closet somewhere, because the information was helpful but their credit is not good enough to get a credit line (patch up your credit while considering partnerships).

Some people have to build up the nerves to write those no money down deals on paper and appropriately present it to the seller. Sometimes they pay five, six, or seven hundred dollars for the books and tapes. And the obtained information is well worth it if you can acquire the patience, motivation, and perseverance for real estate investments. If you have real estate books and tapes put away in your closet; and don't want to spend the money for more books and tapes right now; then you can advertise on the Internet and newspapers that you have real estate books and tapes to

Making Things Happen

either trade or sell. Many real estate professionals do this in order to save money.

This would be a good idea for a beginner investor who wants to work alone or with a partnership while saving money on books and tapes to preserve your money. You will be astonished with the many loopholes and remedies for investing in real estate for as little as no money down.

I just gave the readers another idea that they can add and discuss with the other ideas that will be evaluated at their business partnership meetings. Individuals can work alone with these ideas if desired. These real estate investment ideas can be used by the adults while helping teens learn about smart investments at an early on age. Teens can also use it in their social club if they establish one.

These are some quick tips to help some people who have a hard time getting motivated: a. Write <u>Make-It-Happen</u> at the top of an index card. Then write down some of the ideas in this chapter (along with those you thought up on your own) that motivated you the most and leave that index card or paper on your dresser where you are sure to see it everyday. b. Whenever you are driving, walking down the street, or you're in an office or a particular establishment; pay close attention to the billboards, booklets, windows that promote business phone numbers, and other useful information made available to read about. Write down the phone numbers of advertisements that interest you and call the numbers the first chance you get-then ask that literature on their program be sent to you in the mail.

You need activity other than bills coming in the mail. This new flow of information will enable you to keep generating new ideas for possible business ventures. Join a book club. You can get excellent deals on books from a book club and they will send you listings of their good books every month. Keep educating yourself every chance you get. c. Go to the library-make use of their free use of books, tapes on investments, and other real estate materials. Ask the librarian to direct you to those locations. You can save lots of money and get a free education through the use of the library. d. Take a computer course at the library for free. There are always free Internet courses there. Take information back to your partnership meetings. If you're not in a partnership-then make a folder so you can store your ideas and look at them occasionally. Pretty soon you will have more ideas than you can handle. e. Network, and then exchange ideas with other partnerships.

The Epitome of a Player

This chapter has come to an end; but the next chapter compliments this one. It's not always what you know that will bring you success. Oftentimes it's who you know that will bring you success. The knowledge in this chapter will help you blend in with the influential people who can help you advance in life. You can find them in your players' circle; and I will tell you exactly how to do it.

16

THE PSYCHOLOGY OF
A PLAYERS CIRCLE

I have defined a player as someone who participates in a game or sport. But what are the rules of the game? How will you carry yourself? How will you think and talk? How will you benefit financially? I shall explain these essentials that will formulate: The Psychology of a Players Circle.

The term <u>sport</u> is an old school term on the streets for a person who participates in street game. It was typical for a player to be called a sport during the 1970's and 1980's. How times have changed. I am using this chapter to discuss players who engage in the game for putting projects together for financial gain with the assistance of influential players who they meet in their circle.

The Professional's who can make things happen will know how to recognize each other, interact with each other, and eventually notice how they follow up on their business. Follow up is everything in business if someone has the desire to benefit financially from a project or business venture. What difference does it make if I know someone in an influential position at a bank, but I don't have lunch with this person every now and then? I need to follow up on my acquaintance with the people in that capacity because I never know how I may be able to benefit from them in the future. But at the same time, they need to be able to benefit from me. That's what my folder packed with ideas are for. I will be able to match any benefit they send my way that they can benefit from. One good hand washes the other.

It is important to have your ink pen and your <u>make it happen</u> sheet in front of you to continue writing down ideas as they come to you. I have given you a new skill to use. Take advantage of it by keeping a pen and paper on you wherever you go. Jot down ideas as they come to you. Eventually you will have more ideas than what you need. You will be financially successful with this technique and the ones I am about to discuss with you in this chapter.

You will need to network in order to meet the influential people to help make your projects successful. If you put a business proposal together and then submit it to a financial institution for consideration of a business

The Epitome of a Player

loan, there is some probability that you'll get the loan. But, if I build up a relationship with someone working in a financial institution then submit the business proposal, I should get the business loan because this person knows me and is aware of my efficiency, knowledge, and business skills.

He doesn't know anything about the person he never met who decides to drop a business proposal in front of him. Well what the heck, he is going over that business proposal with a fine tooth comb and research every cotton picking fine print and line on the proposal, because he don't know you from Jack Adams (whoever that is).

The person inside the bank would be just one of the continuous accumulations of people who share the same interest as I do. Now these people will be among my immediate circle along with a widespread circle in many different cities, states, and countries, by use of phone, mail, fax, computers, and person-to-person contacts. This connection and interaction I'm talking about is the player's circle.

In order to be successful in a player's circle-one has to be aware of how to identify that kind of circle-then have the ability to interact with the people involved on a professional, respectable, and sometimes-shrewd manner. This understanding and interaction with the people I'm talking about is called the psychology of a player's circle.

I have already defined the term players circle; and now I'm going to list three definitions of psychology (taken out of Webster's II New Riverside University Dictionary) that I will discuss one at a time, and explain each meaning in regards to how it relates to a players circle:

1. Psychology: The science of mental process and behavior. In this first definition the word science means to observe, identify, describe, and experimental investigation. So, when a person starts interacting in a circle of people who can play the game-an observation to describe how they think and react in given situations, along with an occasional test for final verification, will begin to take place.

It is vital for the player to understand and appropriately speak on what he's about, and be able to back it up in conversation and deed. It doesn't matter if you are working a 9 to 5 job. That's ok. Just make sure you have done your homework. At that point you will be able to talk about and back up the projects you have created on your own because the psychology of the players' circle is to be able to exchange ideas that both parties can benefit from.

The Psychology of a Players Circle

It is never wise to put some of your major innovative programs on the table if you are new to the circle and you're just getting to know a lot of people. Put about one or two small ideas out there (like opening up a Laundromat or a video game room), and see which playmakers send one or two ideas of their own your way. Those will be the <u>prime targets</u> of the first two or three people you interact with in the players' circle.

The feedbacks of ideas you receive don't have to be big projects. You simply need to be able to come up with new ideas to discuss with people in the same or different circle for another exchange of fresh ideas. Remember the last chapter titled <u>Making Things Happen</u>? You need to be able to continuously produce ideas and techniques for legally acquiring money in order to remain as an established player in the circle; otherwise don't step into the mess because sometimes it can stink.

You are basically out of the game if you have ran out of idea's to discuss if the topic comes up. Don't embarrass yourself by trying to hang in the circle if that happens. Disappear and make a showing every now and then until you come up with some new <u>game</u> to talk about. It is ill advised to keep hanging around your players' circle with old ideas because it looks as if you are amateurish in a professional circle-without the ability to keep up. And you definitely don't want that type of rumor floating around about you.

If people are asking why they do not see that much of you-just tell them that you have a couple of business ventures that you're working on, and you will be talking more about it later on down the line. You should give them as little information as possible. You need to keep intrigue in your personality, otherwise; pass the baton and let somebody else run with it. You're out of the race!

2. <u>Psychology: Emotional; and behavioral characteristics of an individual, group, or activity</u>. This second definition of psychology deals with the balance (physically, mentally, and spiritually) that provides emotional stability in a person's character. I stated in the first definition of psychology that a test (experimental investigation) would be applied to one's character occasionally in a particular circle. There are times when an influential person in the position of being able to make financial gain; comes your way; and will test you out in various ways to see if you lose your temper easily. This is an extremely important fact to remember.

Players come in all shapes, sizes, color, creed, nationality and sexes. It could be the little old lady in a business establishment that you

The Epitome of a Player

don't realize have the power or connections to make a check produce for you. She may simply try you out to see how you manage stress and pressure. Many times-influential people want to see you earn your money because success didn't come easy for them, and they may simply feel that you have some dues to pay. Often times, losing your temper can be the mark of a person who is unprepared for success. It is true that losing your temper a little bit will help in certain situations, but the best policy is to keep your emotions balanced at all times (at least until you get to know your associates better).

If you get involved in a partnership of some kind-there will be times when frustrations will surmount, and it would be wise for you to be the organizer, playmaker and peacemaker in those regards. Don't always depend on the supposedly group leader, because that person may not always be around or may be inept at times to appropriately handle an outbreak or uncoordinated circumstance.

Either think of the right words to say or suggest that the meeting be adjourned for another date and time. That will bring a reality check for the group to re-establish controlled temperament and order. Just like you play your way into certain situations; it may be necessary to play your way out at times in order to go back to the drawing board to figure out where you're at in the game, and then what it will take to produce the results you want.

3. <u>Subtle tactical action or argument</u>: In this third definition of psychology: a low-key approach or maneuver may be necessary to bring about the results you're looking for. Sometimes it can come in the form of an argument, but be careful in that area, because you never want to overplay you hand, and you don't want to underplay it. Make sure that you know what's going on and precisely what you will be doing. Otherwise, you will be watching your money float out the window.

A good example is about someone who ran into a businessperson in his player's circle who has ideas in common with his own. Don't panic! He's in your circle. You will see him again. Don't be so quick to approach the man. You need information. Ask some questions. Get on the telephone and make some phone calls. Be well prepared for the conversation. Some influential people like to be introduced by another party. Find out who that other party is. Figure out whether his personality is <u>egotistical, stubborn, relaxed or detailed</u> (E.S.R.D).

The Psychology of a Players Circle

If his personality is <u>egotistical:</u> it will sincerely benefit you to be complimentary on how well behaved his kids are, and how popular his firm or business is. Don't ever over do the compliments; get to your point. Discuss your information and the results of your ideas. If his personality were <u>stubborn:</u> it would be a good point to let him do most of the talking. He will sell himself on you. Only speak when necessary. In most cases he will invite you in on some of his business ventures and ideas. You may even create the makings of a nice friendship.

Remember not to act like an ant dwelling among spiders. Act like a professional who have valuable information (and you do), and ideas-along with a dynamic personality that any professional businessman would be glad to be acquainted with. In other words, do your homework and keep your self-esteem.

If he has a <u>relaxed personality</u>: you can pretty much talk about any kind of subject that sounds good to him. You don't even have to talk about the business subject at all. He will know what you want. Talk about golf, baseball, football, relatives, movies or whatever sounds good. The relaxed personalities just want to be very sociable. At some point and time you can get to business and he will say: "oh sure" that's fine with me.

If he has a <u>detailed personality:</u> you may as well be prepared to do plenty of talking on the business subject alone. He doesn't want to talk about any subject like the relaxed personality. Stick to the point and don't get perplexed if he asks a lot of questions. Detailed people will need a lot of information to be content with you as a person, especially as a business partner.

I need to point out that people should not get confused if someone has two of these personality types because in actuality everyone has two. A person could be egotistical and stubborn with egotistical being the strongest part that comes out the most. So you would sell your personality on his egotistical side. You can be very open minded, and settled, to his stubborn side. A person could be detailed and relaxed, with the relaxed being the strongest part that comes out the most. So you would sell your personality to his relaxed side and be open minded. Simply stay alert for his detailed side when it comes out. Whenever you get a chance read over these four personality descriptions until you know and understand them well. This approach will enable you to make the proper adjustments when necessary.

The Epitome of a Player

At this point it is time to get a folder or a large packet and write: Ideals and Business Ventures on it. Your make it happen sheets will go in the folder along with any numerous amount of paper work that's too much to include on your make it happen sheet. You can also include pamphlets, letters, and any other forms of information that you feel will be beneficial to look at occasionally. I have utilized several boxes of ideas in the past. I always have many ideas to go over. Some worked out for me financially and some didn't. I always throw away the old ideas that didn't work and continue jotting down new ideas and storing them away.

The following hypothetical encounter is an example of a person talking to two playmakers with hopes of making a connection that will bring about an idea for financial gain in this player's circle. Pay close attention to the psychology involved between the three people so that you can imitate or create your own scenario's identical to this one.

The scene is in a restaurant where many people know each other. Michael walks through the door and immediately notices Bill and Sharon eating together.

Michael speaks: "Hello Bill, hi Sharon, how's everybody doing?"

Bill and Sharon happily respond: "Hi Michael (simultaneously)."

Then Bill says: "Hey Mike! Why don't you join us? We haven't seen you around in awhile. What have you been up to?"

Michael is a playmaker but he doesn't know if Bill and Sharon are playmakers. He has seen them on and off over the three months that he's been in this new circle. This is the first time he will be talking to them extensively. Now he is intent on putting some bait out there to see how they will respond.

Michael speaks: "Well, I've been taking college courses, working part time and hanging out in the library every now and then." (Michael has given enough information for them to ask questions and also give a hint if they are playmakers or not).

The Psychology of a Players Circle

Sharon speaks: "Oh! That's very interesting. I've been thinking about taking some courses myself. What are you studying and what's going on at the library?"

Michael's attention is very alert with that response. Sharon is inquisitive, but he will only give enough information to see what feedback he can get.

Michael speaks: "I've been doing some reading in the library about putting a business proposal together and I didn't realize how detailed a proposal can get. Have you any experience with them?"

Michael gives up a little more information, but rather than stop and allow Bill or Sharon to question him some more, he comes back with a question to see if one of them are going to give up some information.

Bill speaks: "I put a business proposal together with a friend-on a pool hall with a game room next to it. Things worked out pretty well for us because customers would go back and forth from the pool hall to the game room. Our competitors started establishing the same type of business in our area and they eventually took most of our customers. They were bigger and had the capital to expand. We didn't; so eventually we had to sell out."

Michael was elated because he ran into some playmakers that were willing to give up some information in order to get some information and maybe become partners.

Michael speaks: "Well, that's interesting, because one of the courses I'm taking in college is finance; and one of my classmates gave me some tapes on banking tactics. Those tapes helped me construct my business proposal on a used car business with a partnership investment office right next to it. The partnerships that we put together will be real estate investment groups that will typically buy multi-unit properties only."
We will give out discounts of fifteen percent on our cars to those people in the partnership, and to those people who rent out units in our properties. In order for us to avoid the mistake of being bought out by our competitors we are going to establish a relationship with 3 banks; besides the bank we get our business loan from. We are going to tell our primary

bank (the bank that gave us the loan) the names of the three banks that agreed to help finance our expansion-provided that we send them a copy of our business financial statement every three months so that they can see the progress we've been making. The contact advisors in the banks will be granted the power to exercise their strategy and business prowess to help us with any unforeseen problems that we may encounter. That will be their way of keeping our business strong and intact-making the facilitation of a loan possible. And that's if, and when we need it.

"Our primary bank will have the names, addresses, and phone numbers of the contact people in the three cooperative banks. They (the contact people in the cooperative banks) will have the name, address, and phone number of the contact person in our primary bank. That way everybody can be in communication and harmony with each other; which will be the makings of an extensive and lucrative business relationship (at this point Michael could offer to exchange phone numbers, and even suggest that they just might be able to do business together, but he want to see the level of their motivation along with whatever their next response will be in order to determine the level of their professionalism)."

Bill speaks: "You know Michael; that is a very elaborate and ingenious business plan you have."

Michael speaks: "Thank you Bill."

Sharon speaks: "Maybe the three of us can set a date and time to meet and then talk about our business plans some more. We may be able to combine our knowledge and resources together; and this could be the makings of a fruitful business association."

Michael speaks: "That sounds fantastic. Here's my phone number. We can talk later on in the week and see what we can set up."

Bill and Sharon speak simultaneously: "That sounds fine Michael." (Bill and Sharon give Michael their phone number).

Obviously, that conversation was between <u>detailed</u> and <u>relaxed</u> personalities. The tempo, mood, and velocity would have been different if there had been one or two of the stubborn-egotistical personalities in the

The Psychology of a Players Circle

discussion. Michael would have had to do more listening than talking with the stubborn person; and he would have had to accommodate the ego of the egotistical personality with a few compliments every now and then. Bill probably spotted a little egotism in Michael when he told him that was a very elaborate and ingenious business plan he has.

Never consider a good conversation with fabulous opportunities <u>as your baby</u>: the idea that's going to change your life for the better. You never know how an idea is going to turn out. Especially when there are other people involved and you don't know how competent they are with following up on an idea and making it work. Many people have enough confidence and drive to start out on a project, but get discouraged when life sends those roadblocks, obstacles, and hard knocks their way.

Many people want everything to go smoothly in a business venture with no challenges or mountains to climb. But what would life be without some challenges, obstacles, and mountains to rise above? Kind of boring, I would think. Have you ever socialized with a person who has no goals, interests, or motivation for getting ahead in life? Try it, but bring a pillow with you so your head won't bump too hard on the floor when you fall asleep on him. It's a terribly boring experience.

Do not focus entirely on your inner circle. In order to come up with different ideas you need to keep doing different things with different people. Try going to a real estate investment seminar. A large quantity of people will be there for you to make small talk with and maybe exchange some ideas and phone numbers with you. That's a good way to find people for partnerships, because you know they will be motivated if they're at the seminar.

You can also ask them if they have any books and tapes at home (on real estate) that they want to sell. If the seminar is full of interesting topics, it won't hurt to buy a set of books and tapes so you can get new ideas to work on; then use as a conversational piece for sharing ideas with other people. You can also trade the books and tapes or sell them at a discount when you're through with them.

Try joining a chess club. Chess players are highly motivated and very calculating people who will have ideas to share. If you run across a chess player who beat you a lot, it would be appropriate and beneficial to humble yourself and ask him to show you where you are going wrong. He will be more than willing to help out; and you will learn a lot more about the game and about yourself.

The Epitome of a Player

Join a book club. You will be able to buy books very cheap and you will be amazed at the numerous listings of interesting books to select from. Even the person who don't like to read will find books that interest him, because the book clubs give a listing of subjects to choose from, and they will send some books on the subjects you selected. You will also get several books for free just for joining.

Remember that knowledge is power; so get started on a reading program right away. Start things out by reading a lot of motivational and inspirational books because that type of literature will pump you up to the point where as you will feel that there is nothing you can't accomplish.

Join a bowling league. You will meet new people and put yourself in a position for new ideas. You will also enjoy the recreation that bowling provides. If you're not getting useful information and you've been on the league for a while; it may be necessary to consider joining a new bowling league (that suggestion is only for the player's that's serious in the game). Remember that you are only searching for information and ideas that will lead you to financial gain, not friendships that produce nothing more than a meaningless periodic conversation. It will be wise when you think about time management and what you're going to get out of a new circle before venturing off into it.

Call a relative that lives in a city where advancement is prosperous and ask the relative questions about opportunities and growth in the city they live in. If the conversation sounds interesting, pay the relative (or friend) a visit for a weekend and find out more about the beneficial areas of the city. If you feel that the city will be well worth the move then do so, or keep it in mind as a place to relocate at during a future date and time.

At this point you should have lots of ideas on your <u>make it happen sheet</u> in your folder that's titled: <u>Ideas and Business Ventures</u>. Don't worry about when or if you will use the ideas. Just get into the habit of jotting down ideas and storing them away. The use of the ideas will come naturally; and that's the basic point I'm making about the psychology of a players circle. The more ideas that you accumulate to socialize about, the stronger you will be inside your chosen circle.

You don't have to keep reading this book right now if you have a strong urge to make some phone calls to start talking to people about the projects and plans that you feel will be successful. It's ok to put this book down for a while and finish it some other time. This book is about getting you started on your innovations and challenges right at this very moment.

The Psychology of a Players Circle

Don't just sit there with your adrenaline rising and you're ready to take action right now. Go ahead and finish writing out some more sentences you wanted to add to your <u>make it happen</u> sheet.

For those who choose to read on: I strongly suggest that you read these two chapters (fifteen and sixteen) over again when you're through with this book. You will be surprised at what you missed along the way; and you will generate even more new ideas than what you already have.

At this point I'm going to summarize the complete definition and understanding of the psychology of a player's circle: I am basically talking about the huge observation of the thinking and emotional control of those people in a circle where ideas (game) are put together in order for you to initiate a low key approach to bring about the desired action or debate that will incorporate financial gain in your life. This means you have figured out how to interact with the playmakers and appropriately meet one or more of them who can be of benefit to you. And of course you have prepared yourself to be of benefit to them by also sharing what you know. The complete purpose of this very skillful interaction is to do so without offending others. Focus on being very professional, polite and respectful.

I have broken down the psychology, the players, and the circle. It's up to you to put all three of them together and make things work for you. Good luck.

17

PEACE AND LOVE

A woman is on her knees flooding a little boy with tears as he lay dead with a bullet in his chest. It's her 6-year-old son. As the shooter's (who missed their targets again) pull away in cars, an elderly woman holds her 78-year-old husband with blood pouring from his right temple (where he was shot). He died in her arms. Was there a gang involved? There are numerous hustlers' who are not gang members that do drive by shootings. Where is the love?

Where is the peace? What if shooters do hit their target? There will be another parent without a son or daughter. Will it be one of our children next? There are players in gangs and there are many who are not in gangs. A gun will fit in all of their hands.

The point I'm making is: **where is the love** on the streets? There is **an appropriate etiquette** on the streets for hustlers (gang members or not) to show **love and respect** for one another. This etiquette goes all the way back to the 1970's when I was a teenager. Gang member's use to call a truce with their rivalries every so often because of too much blood shed, and too many innocent victims getting killed (especially young kids). There haven't been a truce among gang members, players, and hustlers on the streets, in a very long time.

It's about time for a **permanent truce** and a **permanent cease-fire**. Why should hustlers on the streets (gang members and those that's not) keep shedding blood unnecessarily? With all the blood that has been shed from the 9/11 incident, and then the war in Iraq, I would think that it's time for Americans to realize that we (as a people) need to be able to make peace among ourselves before we can effectively make peace in Iraq or any of the other countries. We are long overdue to see **peace** on the streets.

Why can't I come in your neighborhood and why can't you come in my neighborhood? Why are so many of us expressing disgust about the war in Iraq when we keep killing ourselves in the United States?

This definitely seems like a good time to start practicing the proper etiquette of love and respect among us. I would hope that **gang leaders (and those hustlers' on the streets who are not in any gangs) could communicate with each other all over the world and make a strong**

Peace and Love

effort to express a permanent and universal cease-fire all over the world. It would not only make history; it would be a strong showing of our growth, maturity, and professionalism among those who spend most of their time on the streets-in the game.

It would be appropriate if all those players and hustlers in this world who are harboring ill feelings towards another brother in this game (no matter what their race or nationality is), to think about it right now, in regards to how they are going to make amends with that person and show him or her a whole lot of love.

Now don't get up and kick or bang a hole in the wall with your foot or your hand. For crying out loud, it's not that serious and it's not that difficult. Try not to hate the person that bad. Think about it. Think about it for a while and see what happens. You may be glad you did.

Another form of the unspoken etiquette on the streets is that there should be a happy ending to all the madness that you put yourself through on the streets. It doesn't matter how you got out there. We all have a tendency to create our own calamities and obstacles in the game because we never knew how to slow things down and think about the fact that we are supposed to be rising above the mess created by unnecessary killings and careless drug overdoses. Sometimes it's best to go back to the basics.

Why do the streets have to be looked at as a dwelling place for numerous hustlers that struggle getting along with each other? The leaders in their neighborhoods who have control over large groups of people can make miracles happen by getting their people together, and make plans on how they will communicate this universal peace and this universal love. **I'm talking about a permanent truce**. I believe it can happen. **I believe in love** and **I believe in respect. I believe in peace** and **I believe in miracles**. How about you? I am simply the messenger.

The Epitome of a Player

18

HATERS AND BUSTERS

It was around April 1974 when I had just bought a brand new money green 1974 LTD baby Brougham. I was twenty-one years old. I dressed nice, kept butter (perm) in my hair with finger waves, and my nails were always well trimmed and polished. I drove by the corner of 79th and Crandon (the block I lived on) on the Southeast side of Chicago. I use to stand on that very same corner as a teenager, talking to the ladies as they walked by. I knew about the busters, but this was my first experience with real hate

There were three of my buddies standing on the corner. I decided to take them for a spin with me so I pulled to the curb and told them to hop in. There was one riding shotgun and two in the back seat. They had some beer and the usual cheap wine. I passed around two gangster sticks (marijuana joints) to help everybody get mellow. After driving around the neighborhood and kicking it for about an hour, I told them that I had to split and I dropped them off on the same corner I had picked them up on. I was getting out of my car later on that night when I noticed that someone had took something sharp like a razor, and put a nice size slash on my back seat. I was totally caught off guard and practically devastated. I grew up standing on the same corner kicking it with those dudes while we socialized with the ladies as they walked by. We went to the same parties and hung out in the same neighborhoods. So why do me (darn it)?

We shared our teenage years together and our mothers knew us very well, so I couldn't understand why one of them would slash my back seat. This was not the first player hater incident I ran into, but it was the first incident from somebody close to me as a buddy. I had a pretty good idea who it was because there were only two people in the back seat of my car. Many people in our circle disliked the person I had in mind because he was always considered to be loose and petty. I chose not to bring up the incident to anybody I suspected, because they would only point fingers at each other. I dropped the issue and moved on with my life.

Thoughts had flashed through my mind about an incident when I was eighteen walking and socializing with a nice looking young lady. Her girlfriend was walking with her, and it was a mistake for me to allow that to happen because my buddies had schooled me on the fact that a young

Haters and Busters

ladies girlfriend will do something to break up the conversation because of jealousy, hate, or both.

I learned the hard way because that's exactly what happened. Her girlfriend kept butting into our conversation and I had a hard time getting back into the conversation where I finished off. Pretty soon her girlfriend had impolitely taken over the conversation. I excused myself and walked off. Her girlfriend was a professional buster. I had learned a lesson; and believe it or not it happened again a few days later when I started walking and talking to a sweetie pie that had her girlfriend with her. But, I knew what to do this time. I didn't even give her girlfriend a chance to open her mouth. I told the young lady I was talking to that our conversation would be more pleasant and private if we walked by ourselves; so she told her girlfriend to go on without her, and she'll talk to her later. Her girlfriend put a surprise look on her face and left. I felt really good because I didn't want to get burned the same way twice. I even got her phone number.

So behind that incident, along with the back seat of my car getting slashed; I started realizing that I would be running into many player haters and busters. I really felt a need to talk about these two characters because they are everywhere and here to stay.

Even as I put this book together I still run into haters and busters who are typical characters that the professional players in the game will have to continuously rise above in order to live their lives in peace. I will talk about my understanding of both characters-so that those who play the game can simply acknowledge; and then try to stay away from them when they occasionally pop up.

I have come to realize that the haters don't just hate players; but in actuality; they hate anybody who is doing better than them or anybody they simply don't understand. Their problem is within themselves and not other people. Many parents have had to deal with hustlers who beat on their daughters. I said in the Wannabe chapter: they mistake these men for players, and they are not in that category. A professional player is not going to beat on his ladies. He will let them go before sweating himself like that in order to keep a woman who is difficult to get along with. There are simply too many women that will cooperate so why stay on pins and needles with one hardheaded woman?

The professional has enough confidence in himself to replace the difficult ones with somebody else while the unprofessional hustler (who is not a player) acts as if he can't find another woman. They will beat on the

The Epitome of a Player

women they got in order to try and keep them. How foolish can one be? The game is not that serious. Don't make a habit of panicking! The only thing those amateurs are doing is creating haters for themselves and other hustlers who don't deserve to be hated.

In order for a hustler to be the player he wants to be-he will need to rise above the impulse to hit a woman. There are too many men who act as if they entered into a relationship with a gym punching bag instead of a woman. It would be a good idea for some of those women beaters to enter into a relationship with a woman who knows karate so she can fight back and kick his butt. Then he can witness how it really feels to get beat up in a relationship.

The sad point about this hitting is the bragging I have heard from young men about the physical punishment they have gave to a woman, as if they really did something big. Does the man realize that he just finished beating on somebody who was physically weaker than him? And he's aware that he will not pick on somebody the same size as he is. It is the truth. I have taken notice that the men who beat on women are actually cowards who will back down from a real man who will fight them back. There are professional players who should put someone of that nature in check if he hears about a man hitting a woman because it's not necessary and it's bad for the game.

If someone asks the average woman how she feels about a man; he better put his hands over his ears because she may break his eardrums with loads and loads of harsh words about how no good, down right and dirty men are. And she will be right! I grew up with young men who thought they had a gym punching bag instead of a woman. There are too many men creating haters and they need to take a good look at themselves in the mirror and say: I am a <u>dog</u> that needs to change for the best.

I didn't realize at the age of sixteen that I had entered a game where as I would be looked at as a woman beater, and hate from men who would be overly envious of my assets and lifestyle. I hadn't realized how misinformed many people were about a lifestyle that was always meant to be smooth and easy going. Too many deadbeat hustlers have read too many pimp books and have seen too many movies that emulate King Kong. Young people need to realize that those pimp books and movies are the styles of a few players who dictated their own techniques that have played out a long time ago. It was never necessary for them to have the audacity to beat their women as if they are driving cattle out to the pasture.

Haters and Busters

Women are easy to negotiate and reason with. They understand their role in the family. And for those women who have a need to be hit every now and then, I would suggest that the players send them to talk to a psychiatrist to find out what their problem is; because the man shouldn't have to sweat himself that hard for his money. And if that don't help her; just get another one to replace her because she's trouble. And better yet, read over the man of leisure and gentleman of leisure styles that don't use drugs or alcohol. It's a much better lifestyle with more grace and dignity.

Busters are those people who will break up anything a player has going for himself out of envy, spite, or for no good reason at all. Many busters are haters also; and they are typically in the player's way. Busters don't come in the form of just women only; there are male busters also. I was socializing with a male friend over the telephone (in the process of writing this book), and I was telling him about several nice young ladies I had met. He asked if he could meet one of the women I was interested in the most, and I told him no. He got angry and called me a buster. He had plenty of women of his own and I couldn't believe he labeled me a buster because I wouldn't introduce him to a young lady I was interested in.

Men will get in the way of each other for the lust of women. And women will get in the way of each other as busters. How many women can testify to losing her man to her best friend? Yeah, I know quite a few can testify to that. How many men can testify to losing their woman to their best friend? Yep! Quite a few of you can testify to that. What a dog gone cotton-picking darn shame. As many single women and men running around in this world, there are simply too many busters who are too lazy to go out and come up with their own mate. They have to take somebody else's. People who allow others to pull them in another direction are just as guilty as the buster who came on to them. Wasn't their minds made up with the person they originally chose?

Unfaithfulness has created many busters and haters. People should not deny being a buster when they take somebody else's lover. What do you call it when you manipulate, scheme, and then negotiate the getaway plan? Those who have lost someone to another person were fortunate that it happened because it was not going to last long anyway. You now have time to find someone who is a person of his or her word. So what is the point I'm getting at with this entire mess about haters and busters?

From a very spiritual perspective, the game started before the earth was formed. It's not going anywhere. The game was, is, and will always

The Epitome of a Player

be here. Just relax and keep your cool. Give your mind a break. Don't hate the player; don't hate the game. Simply get out of the way or participate.

19

WHERE MEN FAIL

Genesis 3:16-your desire shall be for your husband and he shall <u>rule</u> over you.

Genesis 3:17-cursed is the ground for your sake. In toil you shall eat of it-all the days of your life. Both thorns and thistles it shall bring forth to you.

I have discussed what to do for mental, physical, and emotional balance throughout this book. It is inevitable for me to talk about what is appropriate behavior in a gentleman player's life if he chooses to marry. Many men failed in this area.

It is evident in life that women have done their ordained order (Genesis 3:16) by directing their desires toward man as a husband. But the word <u>rule</u> in the phrase: <u>he shall rule over you,</u> has never been interpreted by man. It has always been his responsibility to interpret the word <u>rule</u> in order to fully understand his relationship with his wife in that area. That's <u>where men fail</u>. Many men also fail to live up to his ordained order to work hard (Genesis 3:17).

During my long quest of making a strong effort to balance out my life spiritually-I read the entire Bible fourteen times. Then I started buying books from a book club on subjects that broke down the different books of the bible for plain interpretation. As I would go through my daily routines of life (to my job, school, and associations with my friends) I did not see evidence of men telling their spouse what to do (marriage is considered to be a virtue of the gentleman of leisure style).

In many cases there were wives who told their husbands what to do. As the years went by while I read the bible repeatedly-I couldn't make sense of the phrase: <u>he shall rule over you,</u> until I recently decided to look the word rule up in Webster's II New Riverside University Dictionary. I was astonished at what I saw. There were thirteen different definitions of the word <u>rule</u>. Which definition would you chose and then address to a woman-this is what it means?

It would be inappropriate for any man to ignore the word <u>rule</u> because it is his ordained order to understand the word and apply it in his marriage with his wife. I thought about this connection being conducted in marriages; then I picked out what I felt was the best interpretation of the word rule, because it's meaning fits in best with the communications in marriages over the years; all the way up to today. It is necessary for the player who will elevate to the gentleman of leisure, to clearly understand his delusion of a rule over women; for spiritual intellect and respect in relationships and marriage with a woman. The following definition is my biblical interpretation of the word rule (out of the 13 dictionary choices).

<u>To keep into proper limits, restrain, and an authoritative direction for conduct</u>. What does this mean? I will explain. At the beginning of time (when only one man and woman was living) a game of deception was played on the woman; then she subjected that deception to man, who in turn, accepted it. The first sin was committed at that point. Neither of them meant any harm towards the other; but to answer that deception; man was given <u>an authoritative direction for conduct-which is to say no to his wife if she is leading him to sin.</u> That will keep the marriage under restraint, and in its proper limits. That is the only <u>rule</u> that man has over his wife (to avoid the sin). Everything else is done by <u>compromise</u> (as evidenced in the world today).

Even though the players' world is outside of biblical boundaries, it is still appropriate and wise to understand (for success in the game) that there are still spiritual implications to their existence and interactions with their women. Mature decisions must be made in order to avoid abuse, add harmony, and then advance to a much higher level. Only certain countries go by the rule factor (their way), but I have doubts about compromising; and did they consider the different meanings of the word rule?

Even in a player's family of women, the man manages the money, bills, and the women; but that was established by compromise. The ladies know that they can leave whenever they choose. I hope that after many men read this chapter they will have a renewed outlook and respect for women, because they are a blessing in the lives of men as companions (and more). It was never meant for man to be alone. He should be mindful and respectful of that fact-no matter what capacity of a relationship he has with a young lady.

There are always issues in marriage such as: who will wash the dishes, who will take out the garbage, who will go to the store, who will do the house cleaning, who will pay the bills, who will wash the clothes,

Where Men Fail

who will watch the kids, who will cut the grass, who will paint the house, who will wash the car, who will walk the dog, and the list goes on.

I will hypothetically discuss a man who enters a marriage with a woman; and then he says that she will do all the house chores and a 9 to 5 job, while he does whatever he wants to do. Her husband will either be carried out the house on a stretcher, or his body parts will be picked up along the highway and put into a bag!

The point I'm making is that one can only go by how the word <u>rule</u> is being applied to the living relationships of today. Many people don't understand the ordained orders of the word <u>rule</u>.

It is man's responsibility to educate hisself spiritually for self-understanding and purpose in life, relationships and marriage. Too many have failed to do so. As a matter of fact: it has been typical for many players to feed their egos by assuming that many women are attracted to them because of their conversation and looks.

Players have failed to realize that women are attracted to them because of an ordained order (Genesis 3:16 verse 3); then for him and the woman, to be husband and wife (the gentlemen's style). This concept establishes the given stipulation for the gentleman of leisure's decision of marriage for his appropriate spiritual balance and spiritual growth for the consolidation of the highest level of a player's game. The man of leisure style is a suitable alternative. The reason why there was an origination of the formulation of pimps and macks: are because of the lack of spiritual understanding of the "he shall rule over you" concept, and the ordained order of women being attracted to men. **The pimps and macks believed it was their looks that pulled the ladies; but to the contrary, it was a biblical ordained order that compelled the ladies attraction to them**.

Is the pimp or the mack "out of pocket" while representing their lifestyles to many women after understanding this breakdown of the "he shall rule over you" concept? Maybe they are out of pocket at this point of my explanation. But, maybe they are not, if at this point (or in the past) the women understood and now understand the "rule" concept, and still agreed to the players terms. Understanding the facts in a compromise is equal to justifying the acceptance. The best way of rectifying the "he shall rule over you" dilemma: is for the pimp or mack to move up to the man of leisure or gentleman of leisure style, or choose the non-male player status until that decision is made. It's a wise choice and mature existence in this intellectual high tech game.

The Epitome of a Player

Why should players stick with a style that is so controversial and highly out-dated? In other words, the pimps and macks can also throw away the bats, sticks and chains, because a sophisticated man can interact with a woman without those beatings. Aren't you tired or sitting on the couch or chair with sweat running down your face while out of breath; huffing and puffing after knocking your woman all over the house and furniture? Isn't that kind of freaked out and crazy? You need a regular job if you're going to work that hard for your money player. The game is not that serious.

In order for the pimp and mack to elevate their style while educating themselves spiritually; and then appropriately applying those principles to their lives: it would be sensible to consider switching to the man of leisure style at first. The gentleman of leisure style could be too difficult for them to make appropriate adjustments to-because that requires more change and change is never easy. Think about it.

I have stated in previous chapters that a man who lacks spiritual wisdom should seek the counsel of someone who does possess spiritual wisdom-along with the patience to help him out. Whoever a man feels is more powerful than him and can give the guidance he need for growth, maturity, balance and wisdom; he should seek that solution with diligence. It could be his karate instructor, his pastor, his mentor, a co-worker, or his soul mate. It's his given choice. He should make a conscious decision in that area if he feels that there is something missing in his life that can make him a better man for a good woman.

Genesis 3:17 Cursed is the ground <u>for your sake</u>. In toil you shall eat of it all the days of your life. Both thorns and thistles it shall bring forth to you.

The curse for man to be hard workers was done for his benefit (<u>for your sake</u>). The definition of <u>sake</u> is: advantage, well, and benefit. Man can only produce success, wellness and intellect, by staying busy (and I don't mean in bed with different women). It has proven to be destructive for men (especially young men) to have too much free time. Whatever a person is looking for out of life will come from hard work.

Man doesn't even have the right to be lazy, because he has an ordained order to work hard and be productive. The phrase <u>both thorns and thistles it shall bring forth to you</u>-is significant of how hard a man should work. Many players are giving up the streets and drugs, but are not sure of what to do next. They are still ordained to work hard. It means to work hard on an honest job for someone else; or you can work hard as an independent contractor or an entrepreneur. That's exactly why I have put such a big emphasis on acquiring a spiritual balance in life; so that many young men will not be walking around talking about: <u>I got to find myself,</u> or <u>I don't know who I am,</u> I need to do some soul searching.

Would you young confused men please give me a dog gone cotton picking break! You guys will go on street corners jacking your slacks (if you can reach them because some of you are wearing pants half way down your rear end), and your mack for a young lady to be a part of your life; and you're not concerned about what the poor woman will think when at some point and time you will tell her: <u>I'm trying to find myself,</u> or <u>I don't know who I am.</u>

<u>Your player status just flew out the window.</u> Do you think the young lady is supposed to tell you who you are or where you should go in order to find yourself? She will definitely know you're having identity problems while stuck on Jupiter and lost in space. It's because you will be standing there trying to rap to her with your pants hanging half way down your rear in, your underwear showing, and a crazy-confused look on your face. But you're hip and in style? Yeah, right.

In other words: pull your pants up first, and then get some spiritual guidance from someone you respect. You will be ready to socialize with a very nice young lady at that point and time. Your conversation just might be believable, and you may even sound as if you finally know who you are.

For many years, even now as I write, I have been seeing too many men conduct themselves as if they are beat down by life. Many men are sleeping on park benches, on the streets, and are walking through alleys looking in garbage cans to see what they can find to eat or sell (some use to be players).

From the very beginning of time man was ordained to be strong, assertive and diligent, with the given ability to work hard and rise above obstacles. It is of the utmost importance that men search their spiritual roots in order to realize and connect to his powerful inheritance of being a successful hard working human being. His strength and wisdom was passed on from generation to generation, but many men lack the wisdom to understand that, along with the drive to back it up.

The spiritual balance is the most important of all the four areas that I mentioned (mentally, physically, emotionally, and spiritually) because

The Epitome of a Player

without it a man will struggle with humbleness in his relationship with his wife or female friend. Humbleness makes forgiveness easier, rather than act out on a woman physically because he can't handle his emotions. It is inappropriate for men to take their uncontrolled anger out on their women, especially if drugs and alcohol is involved. It is mans responsibility to get rid of any narcotics that would hinder his relationship with a woman. It is also his given responsibility to learn and acknowledge that marriage (from a spiritual and gentleman perspective) or friendship is a very reputable and highly significant relationship between a man and a woman that choose an acquaintance together.

Too many young bucks will grit their teeth, bang a hole in the wall, and mumble some crazy cursing words after reading this chapter because it represents change and change can be hard. They were also having what was considered to be their "cake and eat it too" by taking a shower and bath in sex and drugs. They even thought they were going about the game accordingly, even though their style has been out-dated for at least forty years (or more).

There is a failure of knowledge in etiquette and communication for an advanced player to introduce a proficient relationship to a woman (for the gentleman style) that is other than the terms I just mentioned, because that can lead to deception, depression, disputes, arguments and violence. This chapter will benefit teenagers and young adults in a world of many diseases and abusive relationships. It will also help older adults serve as better role models because young people observe how we interact with the opposite sex and emulate us in those areas.

A man intent on being a player should choose the most appropriate style (gentleman of leisure) that is up to date, if not; he will be looked at as being amateurish, uneducated, and behind in the times. Would a clerk look to make a huge amount of money with the same position each year or should he elevate to manager or director? Of course he would elevate, but a definite change in attitude, associations, and values in life, will need to take place also. He will need to take classes for a higher education that compliment his higher position. He will also need to be prepared to make new friends and associations with other managerial staff. The pimp and mack have to make the same adjustments if they want to advance in the game. A good way to start is by putting down the guns and drugs for good.

Many young bucks miss their target the majority of the time while doing a drive by shooting and hit the wrong person. Then they will go and poke that too little to see, peek a boo shame, inside of a woman and make a baby that they won't even own up to. Then they splash in drugs while somebody else pay the baby's bills because they don't want to accept responsibility. We did more than just go out the back door. We came back in, went back out, came back in, and went back out.... Need I say more?

An elevation as a player goes way beyond childish, irresponsible street conduct that has no value for human life. And at the same time, none of the young bucks want a stray bullet to hit one of their brothers, sisters or mothers. Pull off the streets right now before you establish a reputation of being hypocritical, slow to change, with an inability to keep pace among those who are obviously faster and more mature than you are. You know darn well that the majority of young bucks who read this book are still representing yourselves as pimps or macks. Don't even lie about it because those lying bumps on your tongue will get so big-you won't be able to chew your food. Now look at yourself in the mirror and say, "yeah man, I was out there like a bat out of hell." Now don't you feel better? The truth has set you free. Elevate your style and pull up your pants.

By golly! I think you men have got the point. Congratulations to a job well done. Thank goodness I can finally end this chapter. Good luck!

20

LOSERS AND WINNERS

There is no one book that will please everyone throughout this entire world. It doesn't matter who explain positives and negatives in life-to as many people as they possibly can. There will always be a few people here and there that are set in their ways; even if they acknowledge they are living a self-destructive lifestyle. Such is the losers; but the winners listen and make positive changes.

There is an old saying about drugs and alcohol. That saying is: a person who consumes narcotics will do so until he or she is ready to stop-no matter who makes an effort to talk to that person. Many of those people that choose to live life on the edge in the area of stuffing their bodies with illicit substances don't make it to a drug treatment center in time enough to save their lives.

Some people are destined to be losers, because they get so far in a dangerous lifestyle-to the point of not knowing any other way to survive. They live to use drugs and use drugs to live. They are headed towards a dead end street so include them in the circle of losers who can't be helped.

There are those who live by the gun. A weapon in many people's hands gives them a sense of power. Even when they use that weapon to take another person's life-there is a sense of satisfaction and rush that runs through their spine. They actually get to brag to their friends about the person they just shot and killed. Many young people have watched one gangster movie too many. They get some kind of thrill watching the gangster's get out of fancy 1920 cars with machine guns shooting up their enemies-then living to brag about it. There are those young people who rob banks, stores, gas stations, lounges, bars, and any other place that they see in movies. Then they discuss it with their friends who end up being an accomplice.

There are those who rob dope houses, crap games, and people who are dressed in suits that look like they have plenty of money in their pockets. I may as well mention that many of those robbers get killed while trying to rob a bank or a lounge or a dope house…. I will add them to the list of losers who make bad decisions in life.

No matter what I say about a man being respectful to women and treating them like ladies-there will still be some men who beat on women

Losers and Winners

because they are barbaric cowards and have no discipline. Add to the list-the many men who organize a family of women to put on the streets for pandering, because they are behind in the times and lost in the game.

Let's not forget about the men who have three or four girlfriends, because they are caught up in lust and have no spiritual balance in their lives. Many men in that category will be too lustful to stop. There will always be many men that will not take care of their kids. They want to make babies without the responsibility of taking care of them (as if love making is a play station), and women get stuck with the kids because they thought that they were dealing with a real man. He simply turned out to be a little boy who just wanted a toy and some Lego blocks to play with (don't forget his baby bottle in the future).

Even the many women who do marry a man that's balanced out evenly (mentally, physically, emotionally, and spiritually) still get stuck with some as a dead beat, because he didn't stay balanced in those areas year after year after year. There should be no slack in the balance-whether it is on the woman's part or the man.

Let's say a woman's husband of five years decided to stuff his well-built body with anything that's put in front of him. He blows out to 350 pounds at 5 feet 7 inches tall. He has given up his spiritual reading and practice; then he stopped going to the gym (because he has her). This leaves the woman stuck with a big roly-poly slob who sits in front of the television the majority of the time with a sandwich in both hands and a pitcher of beer next to him. He will even have the audacity to stay mad at her because she won't make love to him anymore. I wonder why?

Losers come in all shapes, sizes, and all walks of life. It is up to the man and the woman to stay focus on a well-balanced lifestyle; otherwise, they will be miserable to the point of no return. They will need the ability to change and make some appropriate adjustments like the suggestions I have given throughout this book.

I have chosen not to use up too much paper talking about losers. I prefer to get straight to the point with the winners. It's a more pleasant subject. The definition of winner is: one of exceptionally superior quality or character. The following ten statements are good descriptions of what winners do:

1. Winners stay away from drugs, alcohol, and cigarettes. They realize that those illicit substances don't make a person hip or cool.

The Epitome of a Player

In actuality, those substances kill-not heal. They are content with being themselves and leaving it up to others to accept them for who they are (or find another friend).

2. Winners are cool in school and will stay in school and continue their education. They realize that mastermind groups, computers, downsizing, empowerment and facilitation, has made employment very competitive, and they do what it takes to survive in a constant fast pace; fast changing world.

3. Winners are positive people who will only associate with positive people that avoid the use of drugs or alcohol. They focus on doing honest and legal business ventures to survive and enjoy life. They are very enjoyable people to be around and will be there for you in times of trouble. They are dependable.

4. Winners understand the value of change and adjust to it very well. They believe in going to different neighborhoods to meet new people who have new and constructive ideas. If they like a new area or new city they will move there because change is power. They understand that very well. They are survivors who do what it takes to make the appropriate adjustments whenever necessary. They are the go-getters and the people who get things done. If you ever want something done right just ask a busy person, who is of course, the winner.

5. Winners are humble people who are not afraid to ask for help. It takes an acceptance of humbleness and humility to make it in life. Winners understand that and made it a part of their personality.

6. Winners know the importance of a savings program and do well in that area. It is always good to have money put away for unexpected emergencies and to help with school expenses.

7. Winners meditate and exercise for physical strength, stamina, and emotional control.

8. Winners don't follow-they lead.

9. Winners don't wait around for opportunities to happen-<u>they make it happen</u>!

10. Winners are in charge of their life. The final decision is always theirs. Life doesn't kick them in the butt. They kick life in the butt. They move mountains, cross-deserts, and swim the deepest sea. They do what it takes to make it in life. You are a winner!

This chapter, along with all the other chapters in this self-help motivational book, has provided more than enough useful information, inspiration and motivation, to make a change towards a lifestyle that will benefit any reader. I didn't just touch on the subject of drugs and alcohol. I have also discussed the violence in relationships, along with the reasons on why people make ill-advised decisions during everyday courses of activity in their lives.

There is substantial power in this book. The power to change and be the winner you was meant to be. The power to change and be the player you was meant to be. The power to change and be the non-player you was meant to be. It's your choice and your ballgame. You are the one hitting the home runs. Nobody can swing the bat better than you can swing it for yourself.

Don't let the information provided in this book go to waste. At this point and time you should be knocking people down to get to drug treatment facilities. The next step is to register in schools-then go to libraries and bookstores to obtain more inspirational, informative, and motivational books. Don't let the losers keep feeding you that poison to put in your body! It only gives an illusion of happiness, but your situation is actually worse because you spent all your money. When you sober up, you start thinking about bills that need to be paid, utilities have been disconnected, and you're just that close to being evicted.

To make matters worse; you are either short on food or completely out of food. The kids are hungry; you don't know which way to go; and you don't really care because you got one more bag of dope left. In other words, you have freaked out! You have been on Pluto long enough. Get off that planet and return to Earth.

Get up right now and do what it takes to bring a positive change in your life. Start kicking life in the rear end-rather than you allowing life to

The Epitome of a Player

keep kicking you in the rear end (and you know I'm right). You're the one that's in charge of your life and your destiny. You are the answer! You are the winner who can and will start making positive things happen in your life.

I need to stop writing right now so I can start making preparations to get out of your way-in order to keep from getting ran over while you zoom down the road to success. Good luck you dog gone winner you!

SUMMARY

The intent of this book is to save lives by providing knowledge, direction, purpose, and discipline, needed in the areas of street hustle and relationships (then enhance job careers and balance in life). It doesn't take a strong effort to watch the news on television, read newspapers, and walk through neighborhoods going to school, going to work, going to the store or wherever; in order to know that society has an enormous problem with illegal drug activity. Prostitution, unemployment, affordable health care, marriages and courtship, are also problems to be addressed.

We learn from books and other people. Writers help people by sharing their knowledge and experiences in the form of a book. It's up to the readers to make use of any valuable information that can make a wise, positive, and constructive change in their lives.

Society has many problems with crime, violence, and ineffective decision-making (because of a lack of balance in life) that start at an early age. This dilemma starts as early as eleven or twelve years old. Many girls are getting pregnant as young as ten, eleven, and twelve years old. In too many cases there are no fathers around to accept responsibility for their kids (but they either wanted a father or were glad to have a father around when they were kids). More young men should step up and accept their role as the father of their children; because it's obvious that the sex was good, so the woman and the baby are good for you too. Be mature; and most of all, be a man.

There is the age-old problem of physical abuse to women and men in courtship and marriage. Are we as parent's (along with the schools) waiting too long to come up with a system/program-that will prepare our children for courtship, marriage, and a responsible well balanced lifestyle at the adolescent age or sooner? If we as parents, school authorities, and other relatives; don't help the kids out at an early age; their peers will. Doesn't that sound spooky?

A very popular first lady made a statement that: <u>it takes a village to raise a child</u>. Everybody plays a part; such as the uncles, cousins, brothers, sisters, fathers, mothers, teachers…. I talked about role-playing for the children in grammar school (at least by the age of eleven) in order to help prepare them for the appropriate responses in disputes during courtship, friendship and marriage.

The Epitome of a Player

Preparation at an early age will help our kids avoid physical abuse later on in life. Why keep shipping women to shelters for battered women when a system can be developed for them at an early age-that will help them stay calm, mature, and less temperamental when negativity arises in relationships with the opposite sex?

Our teenagers will continue to tiptoe out to places for sexual gratifications with the opposite sex if they don't foresee a future marital or friendship bond between the ages of eighteen and twenty-two. That doesn't mean they have to get married around those ages. It will simply provide visualization at a determined and appropriate time frame for sex, love, and companionship. Our children are more advanced and prepared for lovemaking and accepting responsibility-than many parents realize. A respectable, humble approach, to discussing those concerns with them would be the noble and adult decision under those circumstances.

In many cases children will not feel compelled to run away from home, commit suicide, and sneak around to have sex if parents will be open minded to being a friend to their kids and allowing them to talk about anything and everything without the parents losing their temper.

Our kids want to be able to come to their parents and discuss their concerns (whether intimate or not). In many cases they are afraid of getting scorned, rejected, misunderstood, beat, and often times; put on a punishment. No wonder kids hold things in and then release them in the wrong way.

I talked about the different styles of players so that young people could have more than the pimp and mack style to choose from. Those two styles are very old, unscrupulous, and have basically played out. The man of leisure and gentleman of leisure styles are elevated and professional-without the use of drugs, alcohol, and cigarettes. You are a better decision maker with your life at those two levels and know better than to put illicit substances in your body that can kill you.

It is also notable to understand that you can represent yourself as a non-male or non-female player. You can be successful in life with no titles at all. The choice is yours, but be responsible; and make wise, mature decisions about your physical and mental wellness.

I felt a need to clarify the ordained order of <u>rule</u> as it was issued to the first man and woman on the earth. The word rule has many different meanings and it's highly inappropriate to use that word in a way that's contrary to everyday living.

Summary

Women are not slaves to men. It would be erroneous for a man to enter a relationship with a woman and have the false misconception that he can order a woman around. I am basically clarifying that assumption in order to keep men from going to <u>their funerals</u> before their time.

Women were created as companions for men; because it was never meant for man to be alone. A man can accomplish a lot in life with the strong, positive energy; which derives from the love, companionship, and support from a woman.

Whether hustlers on the street realize it or not; there are suppose to be a happy ending to the mistakes and misfortunes that brought misery and struggle in our lives. There are always obstacles to rise above in life, but in many cases we as a people create our own obstacles with tragedies and disillusions during the course of a lifetime.

We have the ability to create our own heaven on earth. **This seems to be an excellent time for gangs, hustlers, and players, to organize a permanent cease-fire and truce throughout the world.** Many lives have been lost because of the September 11, attacks-along with the war in Iraq. Why keep shooting at one another and taking more lives along with those of innocent bystanders such as little children and other loved ones?

This is a time for Americans to pull together as a people and show sincere love for each other. Then we can communicate that love to other countries rather than fight first and talk later. Our soldiers shouldn't have to come home to war on the streets after fighting for their country. The streets, our kids, and loved ones, will be safer when those who pick up guns-put them down and be positive role models instead of killers.

The bad doesn't have to stay ugly. The thought is the cause of it all and knowledge is the key to unlock those doors of success in every aspect of ones life. <u>Knowledge</u> is power; and this book is the beginning of the realization of that power in the lives of many people. This book is the beginning of the road for many people to continue their reading related material that will mode and build strong, positive relationships, with a successful attitude and position in life.

I have just taken a paintbrush and started painting a picture. Now I am handing the brush over to you. Finish the picture. You're a much better artist of your life than I am. No one can paint a better picture than you.

The Epitome of a Player

GLOSSARY

1. Bottom woman: The fastest, most loyal, and biggest go-getter of the money than any other woman in a player's family.

2. Butter: A street slang for perm in a player's hair.

3. Celli: A cellmate in a penitentiary.

4. Fancy man: An old school term for a player in the game.

5. Flip side: Another side of a story.

6. Foxy: To talk hip. 2. An attractive woman.

7. Gangster stick: Marijuana joint.

8. Godfather hit: A big chunk of cocaine put on a pipe to smoke.

9. In the mix: Associating with people who have common interest in a very fast circle.

10. Jack your mack: Hype up your conversation with a woman. Real smooth and direct. A player's rap to a woman.

11. Jack your slacks: Pull up your pants with both hands in a cool motion while socializing. A man does it as a sign that he is a player.

12. John: Trick or date. A person who solicits sex for pay.

13. The joint: Street slang for the penitentiary or for a neighborhood jailhouse.

14. Kick it (kicking it, kicking live game) a cool way to say lets socialize or we're socializing.

Glossary

15. Kicking live game: A heavy conversation about ideas for making money and the latest happenings in the circle. Typical street slang.

16. Lid cocked ace duce to the side: A brim (dress hat) leaning forward and to the side of a person's head. A typical player or gangster style.

17. Macking: A street term for a player who has the gift of being an exceptional talker to women.

18. Packing: Carrying a gun.

19. Playmaker: A street term for a player in the game who has the ability to create ideas and make a successful financial gain from one or more of those ideas.

20. Riding shotgun: Sitting in the front seat (passenger side) of a car with a shotgun to do a drive by shooting.

21. Shooting the breeze: (shoot the breeze) a cool way to say you are socializing with a hip crowd (old school).

22. Speed: Amphetamine and Meth-Amphetamine.

23. Spit that game: Talk very cool, hip, and knowledgeable, about fast living.
24. Sporting lady: (sport-n-lady) a fancy name for a street hooker in a player's family.

25. Try their hand: Street slang for trying out a game that's played on the streets; like pimping, macking, or dealing drugs.

26. Wheel and deal: Dealing drugs or trying to be slick about a game you are playing on the streets or in a business transaction.

27. Young bucks: Young players or young street hustlers.

The Epitome of a Player

About The Author

Ernest Ivy II was born January 19, 1953 at Cook County Hospital in Chicago Illinois. He has an only son, Ernest Ivy III. He has three brothers, two sisters, and his mother.

During the publication of this book he has spent the last eight years in Joliet (the city of hope) Illinois. In 1971 he attended Lakeland College in Sheboygan, Wisconsin. His major was business administration. Some of the courses that he studied were: Introduction to Logic, Introduction to Psychology, Sociology and Humanities. He served in the U.S. Navy.

He went to school for real estate sales and real estate brokerage at Real Estate Education Company and The Chicago Board of Realtors between 1986 and 1987. He worked out of five different real estate offices as a real estate salesperson and then a real estate broker.

Writing took precedence in his life when he started writing short stories in grammar school. Then, around 1979, he started writing poetry as a hobby and eventually started putting a manuscript together about poetry. He stopped writing poetry in order to write The Epitome of a Player at a later date to help our young people on the streets avoid drive by shootings, drugs, and other mistakes players and hustlers make. This was done for the sole purpose of helping them avoid violence and making adjustments in a new life after the fast lane is gone.

The most difficult aspect of playing the game has been for hustlers to show love towards one another by talking things out, rather than pick up the guns to shoot each other down. But, the love and talking things out- have to be done in order to achieve professionalism and respect in a game from the old school.

Put the guns down and master the difficult part of the game (force yourself if you have to) by showing the love that use to be there, and has to come back between us. The leaders on the streets in the neighborhoods where the shootings are going on-can be major players in enforcing this love-so that the shootings can stop permanently. That move will return respect back to the game. Just think about it. We don't owe it to anybody except ourselves. Peace and love to you, my friend.

The Epitome Of a Player

By

Ernest Ivy II

www.ingramcontent.com/pod-product-compliance
Lightning Source LLC
Chambersburg PA
CBHW051756040426
42446CB00007B/393